Warrior • 92

OSPREY
PUBLISHING

US Marine Corps Tank Crewman 1941–45

Pacific

Kenneth W Estes • Illustrated by Howard Gerrard

First published in 2005 by Osprey Publishing
Midland House, West Way, Botley, Oxford Ox2 0PH, UK
443 Park Avenue South, New York, NY 10016, USA
Email: info@ospreypublishing.com

A CIP catalog record for this book is available from the British Library

ISBN 1 84176 717 4

Editor: Katherine Venn
Design: Ken Vail Graphic Design, Cambridge, UK
Index by Alan Thatcher
Originated by Grasmere Digital Imaging, Leeds, UK
Printed in China through World Print Ltd.

05 06 07 08 09   10 9 8 7 6 5 4 3 2 1

FOR A CATALOG OF ALL BOOKS PUBLISHED BY OSPREY MILITARY AND
AVIATION PLEASE CONTACT:

NORTH AMERICA
Osprey Direct, 2427 Bond Street, University Park, IL 60466, USA
E-mail: info@ospreydirectusa.com

ALL OTHER REGIONS
Osprey Direct UK, P.O. Box 140 Wellingborough, Northants, NN8 2FA, UK
E-mail: info@ospreydirect.co.uk

Buy online at www.ospreypublishing.com

Artist's note

Readers may care to note that the original paintings from which the color plates in this book were prepared are available for private sale. All reproduction copyright whatsoever is retained by the Publishers. All inquiries should be addressed to:

Howard Gerrard
11, Oaks Road
Tenterden
Kent
TN30 6RD
UK

The Publishers regret that they can enter into no correspondence upon this matter.

Author's Acknowledgments

The author is indebted to many individuals, beginning with my key to USMC veteran tankers, retired Master Gunnery Sergeant Donald R. Gagnon. Barry Zerby and Trevor Plante of the Military Records sections rendered the most essential services of the National Archives and Records Administration. At the USMC Historical Center, Washington DC, I received expert assistance from Danny A. Crawford, Robert V. Aquilina, Lena M. Kaljot, and Evelyn A. Englander. I am indebted to Ken Smith-Christmas, Dieter Stenger, Mark Henry, Keith Alexander and Al Hinde of the USMC Museums Branch, Quantico, Virginia, for their assistance in researching weapons, equipment and clothing. All photographs are from the National Archives, the Marine Corps Research Center, the Museums Branch, and the author's collection. Jacques Littlefield and Mark Green assisted me with details and a visit to the Military Vehicle Technology Foundation operated by Mr. Littlefield. Also assisting me were Oscar E. Gilbert, Steven J. Zaloga, Daniel Shepetus, Robert M. Neiman, Edward L. Bale, Benjamin W. Pugsley, William F. McMillian, Granville G. Sweet, Louis B. Metzger, and Rowland Hall. The character of Fred Crowley is completely fictitious, representing a composite of the World War II Marine Corps tanker, however the events depicted are all historical, once "Fred" reaches his tank unit.

CONTENTS

INTRODUCTION   4

CHRONOLOGY   5

ENLISTMENT   7

TRAINING   10
Tank school • After tank school

APPEARANCE AND DRESS   17
Prewar uniforms • New uniforms for the Pacific war • Tank crew garb in combat

BELIEF AND BELONGING   22

ON CAMPAIGN   24
Early "tanking" in the Marine Corps • The Marine Corps tank • The tank park routine
To the 'ville • Into battle • Learning to fight • Veteran tankers in action

THE AFTERMATH   57

MUSEUMS AND COLLECTIONS   59

BIBLIOGRAPHY   60

COLOR PLATE COMMENTARY   60

INDEX   64

US MARINE CORPS TANK CREWMAN 1941–45 PACIFIC

INTRODUCTION

"OK Crowley, I've got you this time, you screwed up one time too many … Report to the Commanding Officer!" the first sergeant barked. Private first class (PFC) Fred Crowley marched into the office of Captain Richards, the CO of B Company, 6th Marine Infantry Regiment. The captain looked at the record and the charges filed by the shore patrol in nearby San Diego, showing how this misfit had once again brawled in the bars and resisted apprehension, and sworn at the corporal in charge. "I've seen enough of you, young man, I don't want your kind in my outfit. I'm dismissing the charges, but only so I can transfer you. First sergeant, send this man with the other three to battalion, on the quota for the tank unit." Turning to Crowley, he growled, "You're going to be a grease monkey now, see how you like that! Dismissed!"

Fred, who had joined the Marine Corps only two years before, after leaving his birthplace of Grant's Pass, Oregon, to seek travel and a paid job, now found himself ousted from his comfortable home in 1st Battalion, 6th Marines, where he had been a rifleman in B Company. Now, on May 5, 1941, he found himself heading, with several dozen other rejects, to 4th Tank Company, Fleet Marine Force (FMF), now known as A Company, 2d Tank Battalion and part of the new 2d Marine Division, which was standing up with hundreds of newly trained and transferred men arriving daily since formally organizing that February.

Marines had adopted tanks in their organization after they decided on the mission of forcible entry against beaches defended by a determined and well-armed enemy. This mission would be at the center of a naval campaign, which would at the same time require other Marine Corps units to defend islands and coastlines against similar all-out assault. They had experimented with borrowed M1917A1 light tanks beginning in 1923. A tank platoon deployed to China 1928–29, but was disbanded upon return.

In 1934, the Marine Corps planned two tank companies of 5-ton light tanks for its two brigades proposed for duty in

What the Marine Corps sought in its tanks in 1940 was this: a Marmon-Herrington CTL-3a light tank, or tankette, weighing not more than 5 tons for ease of handling, able to land with the amphibious assault and knock out the machine guns of the beach defenders and support the advance inland, supplied by the LVT-1 amphibious tractor. (USMC photo)

the Atlantic and Pacific fleets. The vehicle selected was the two-man Marmon-Herrington CTL-3. The Marine Corps bought a total of 35 Marmon-Herrington tanks, but the coming of World War II required adoption of army light and medium tanks for a variety of reasons.

Marine Corps tankers then operated M2A4 and M3 light tanks. After February 1944, all USMC landings would feature the M4 series medium tanks. Marines officially first used the flame-thrower tank on Saipan to flush the enemy from caves. Earlier, tankers had improvised flame weapons for light tanks. On Iwo Jima, tank bulldozers were employed to seal enemy bunkers. At the end of the Battle of Okinawa, Major-General Lemuel Shepherd wrote in his after-action report that "if any one supporting arm can be singled out as having contributed more than any others during the progress of the campaign, the tank would certainly be selected."

Just as the amphibian tractor changed in its Marine Corps role and mission, the tank, by late 1943, was fighting other tanks, antitank guns, infantry, artillery and fixed fortifications. No longer used as an independent unit, as at Guadalcanal, tank companies and platoons fought in close coordination with the infantry to blind, burn and blast, "processing" the enemy-held territory yard by yard. By the war's end, demands for even larger and more powerful tanks came from tankers and senior commanders alike, including General Lemuel Shepherd, a later commandant, who as a Lieutenant-Colonel in 1939 had urged the Corps to acquire standard army-type tanks.

Along the way, marines made several key innovations, including the improvisation of tank infantry telephones and flame-throwers (1943), the use of diesel-powered tanks overseas (1943), the use of pontoons to float tanks ashore in amphibious assaults (1945) and the first use of Sherman flame tanks (1945). Many other field improvisations occurred in individual units. Marine tankers bore much deprivation in far-off places and in cruel combat against a determined and fanatical enemy. In the end, victory came because, as Lieutenant-General Mitsuru Ushijima, commanding the Japanese 32nd Army on Okinawa, put it: "The enemy's power lies in its tanks."

CHRONOLOGY

1923   The commandant general approved the crucial study *Advance Base Operations in Micronesia* as the main Marine Corps operations plan
December 5, The light tank platoon, Marine Corps Expeditionary Force, formed at Quantico, Virginia, with a strength of two officers, 22 men, and three M1917A1 6-ton tanks borrowed on oral agreement from the army

1927   **April 6**, The light tank platoon departs for Tientsin, China, and duty with the 3d Marine Expeditionary Brigade. Upon return, it disbands on November 10, 1928

1937   **March 1**, 1st Tank Company, 1st Marine Brigade, formed at Quantico. It is later redesignated 1st Scout Company

1940   **July**, Congress approves the "two-ocean" navy-building program
November 1, 3d Tank Company, 1st Marine Brigade, and 4th Tank Company, 2d Marine Brigade, formed

1941   **February 1**, 1st and 2d Marine Divisions formed with 1st and 2d Scout Companies, 3d and 4th Tank Companies
July 4, Tank Company (now A Company, 2d Tank Battalion) deployed with the 1st Provisional Marine Brigade to garrison Iceland
November–December, 1st and 2d Tank Battalions formed in their respective divisions

1942	**January**, B Company, 2d Tank Battalion, detached for duty in with the 2d Marine Brigade guarding Samoa
	June, 1st and 2d Separate Tank Companies form on the east and west coasts to man the Marmon-Herrington tanks rejected by the tank battalions. These are later dispatched to Samoa to relieve two tank companies, which rejoin their tank battalions
	July, Tank School, FMF Training Center, Camp Elliott (San Diego) established
	August 7–9, USMC tanks in combat, landing at Guadalcanal and Tanambogo Island, Solomons (A and B Co. 1st Tk. Bn., C Co. 2d Tk. Bn.)
	September 16, 3d Tank Battalion formed
1943	**January 18**, 1st Corps Medium Tank Battalion formed
	May 12, 4th Tank Battalion formed
	July 15, Tank platoons of 9th, 10th, and 11th Defense Battalions in action at Munda Island
	September 16, Tank platoons of 9th, 10th, and 11th Defense Battalions in action at Arundel Island
	November 1, Assault landing at Cape Torokina, Bougainville Island (3d Tk. Bn.)
	November 20, Assault landing at Betio Island, Tarawa (2d Tk. Bn., C Co., 1st Corps Medium Tk. Bn.)
	December 26, Assault landing at Cape Gloucester, New Britain (1st Tk. Bn.)
1944	**January 3**, 5th Tank Battalion formed
	February 1, Assault landing on Roi-Namur Island, Marshalls (4th Tk. Bn.)
	February 18–22, Assault landing on Eniwetok Atoll (2d Sep. Tk. Co.)
	June 15, Assault landing on Saipan (2d and 4th Tk. Bn.)
	July 21, Assault landing on Guam (3d Tk. Bn., 2d Sep. Tk. Co., 4th Marines Tk. Co.)
	July 24, Assault landing on Tinian (2d and 4th Tk. Bn.)
	September 15, Assault on Peleliu Island, Palaus (1st Tk. Bn.)
	October 1, 6th Tank Battalion formed
1945	**February 19**, Assault on Iwo Jima (3d, 4th and 5th Tk. Bn.)
	April 1, Assault on Okinawa (1st and 6th Tk. Bn.)
	September 3, V-J Day

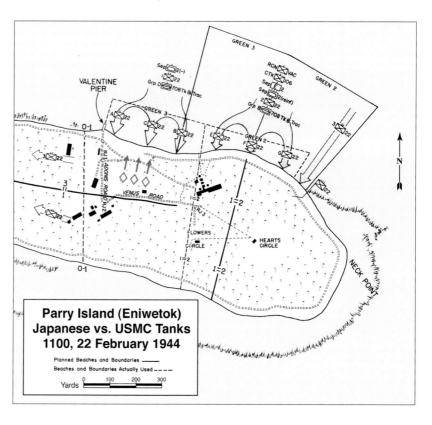

Parry Island (Eniwetok) Japanese vs. USMC Tanks 1100, 22 February 1944

Planned Beaches and Boundaries ———
Beaches and Boundaries Actually Used – – – –

Yards   0   100   200   300

The first standup fight between USMC and Japanese tanks fell to the men of the 2d Separate Tank Company on Parry Island in the Eniwetok Atoll. Three Type 95 light tanks charged the beachhead, much to the surprise of all, but they were quickly overwhelmed by the firepower of USMC M4A2 tanks. (Map by W. Stephen Hill from US Army original)

September 1945–46, North China operations (1st and 6th Tk. Bn.)
1946   **March 26,** When 6th Tank Battalion disbands, only 1st and 2d Tank
Battalions remain on active duty, where they continue to the present day

ENLISTMENT

There were as many reasons for a man to join the US Marine Corps as there were recruits. The tall, trim recruiting NCOs, immaculately turned out in their dress blue uniforms, could be found in neighborhood recruiting offices, and made frequent visits to schools and public gatherings, always alert for a volunteer or just a person in life's transition. Once the seemingly endless paperwork was filled out amid a flurry of questions, it could be just a matter of days before a train or bus ticket was produced and the new recruit was on his way to one of the two recruit training depots ("boot camps") maintained by the Marine Corps at San Diego, California, and Parris Island, South Carolina. Over the near-century of their dual existence, much scuttlebutt has been spilled over the differences in the training and rigor of the two depots. One general often put it this way: "… there *is* one difference. At San Diego they teach recruits, when jumping off a sinking ship, to hold their nose. At Parris Island they teach them to hold their private parts. So, the only way to know for sure where a marine was trained is to wait until he jumps off a sinking ship."

Fred Crowley had joined the Marine Corps in December 1938, two years before the National Emergency call-up of reserves and another before the Pearl Harbor attack produced a wave of volunteering and Selective Service inductees. The Marine Corps then mustered just over 19,000 officers and men. When the war started, it would already have over 70,000, on its way to the wartime peak of 458,053. More marines would serve during World War II than had joined the Corps in its entire history before 1941. The terms "Old Corps" or "Old Breed," later attached to Fred and his brethren, thus applied to a mere 3 percent of the wartime USMC. Years later, Fred would talk about his early life:

> I imagined in 1935 – after seeing a movie – that I wanted to be a cowboy. But then it was back to school, not that they could teach me anything. I spent most of my time telling the other kids how I learned to roll a smoke. I did get the years in and graduated from grammar school! Principal Wilson held up my diploma until I got $5 to pay for a window I broke.
>
> It was then that I learned about the CCC [Civilian Conservation Corps] Camps. It was about one day after that I signed my mother's name and was off to Vancouver Barracks, Washington, boot camp to become a CCC boy at the tender age of 15. I got $5 a month, and my mother received $25. My mother had been mad as hell until she knew where I was, as she thought I was on the bum. The money she was getting each month enabled my brothers to stay in high school. I spent two years in the CCC Camp in Humbug Mountain, Oregon, Silver Creek Falls, Oregon, and finished up at Silver Creek, Michigan, where I received a Dishonorable Discharge. I thought that was the end of the world. Later, when I signed my life away to the Marine Corps and told my recruiter about the discharge, the Sergeant said, "You

should be proud of it. I took a $3.50 cut in pay when they started that damned outfit!" Which reminds me of the Sunday at home when I was leaving for the Marine Corps Boot Camp at San Diego ... My mother said to my Uncle Tom (a WWI Veteran), "He will be nothing but a bum!" to which my Uncle responded, "Yes, Irene, he will be a bum, but a damn good bum." That now turns out, was pretty true about my life ... "A Damn good bum!" Back in the 30s, boot camp was tough, but depression kids were tough too, so we had no problems with it. Just as long as they fed us we could put up with anything. I was in the 6th Marines when Gunny Sergeant Martinez selected ten of us for sea duty, so after sea school graduation I was sent to the USS *Nevada*. I took a train from San Diego to Seattle, Washington. My ship was at Bremerton Navy Shipyard. In those days you took your sea bag, rifle, bayonet, and one clip of ammo (five .03 rounds). Somewhere along the line, years later, they didn't trust a marine with his rifle ashore. It was about this time, 39 or 40, that the old 'squad right, squad left' drill method came to an end. As my old 1st Sgt. R. R. Inks used to say in disgust, "Fall in like three rows of corn!" Right around the same time we had to give up our Model 1903 rifles and were issued the Ml Garand. The old-time marine had a fit. I was just a boot and I could roll with the punches. At that time we had corporals with ten years in grade and they didn't adjust well with all the changes. I should have extended six months on board ship to make corporal. Salt-water promotions had to be held for six months before they were good in the infantry.

Fred came back to the 6th Marines in 1940, but eventually ran afoul of the shore-type discipline. Some NCOs really had it in for him in B Company of the 1st Battalion of the 6th Marines, the only regiment then in California. But in a time of expansion and barely organized chaos, his company commander had an easy way to transfer his problem. He placed Fred on a quota for another 2d Marine Division unit forming in the summer of 1941.

The boot camp experience of 1938 really was suited to the times. Physical violence seldom happened, and the drill instructors used their impressive vocal talents to urge the recruits through their drills, hikes, and exercises. They taught their charges the tradition and customs of the Marine Corps, using a simple shorthand history to regale them with storied examples of past heroism, toughness, and endurance. Above all, the recruits learned to handle weapons and shoot them – and shoot well. They also learned the peculiar nomenclature of the naval service, and shipboard life in particular. As many have observed, marines can be seen as sailors who swear a lot. One of the important events for each recruit was the issue of his uniforms and the individual equipment he would use in the field. Called "782 gear" from the issue receipt document, it included the web gear, packs, pouches, canteens, and so forth that the unit considered he must have. In Fred's time, the rifle, Model 1903, .30 caliber, would also be issued to the marine, to be turned into the unit armory upon arrival as he changed from station to station.

After the war began, recruits and marines learned a credo to accompany the Corps' almost manic approach to precise marksmanship training. Much later, Fred could still recite it to his grandchildren. The first half reads:

> This is my rifle. There are many like it, but this one is mine. My rifle is my best friend. It is my life. I must master it as I must master my life. My rifle, without me, is useless. Without my rifle, I am useless. I must fire my rifle true. I must shoot straighter than my enemy who is trying to kill me. I must shoot him before he shoots me. I will ... My rifle and myself know that what counts in this war is not the rounds we fire, the noise of our burst, nor the smoke we make. We know that it is the hits that count. We will hit ...

The pay scale and rank structure of the Marine Corps had been aligned to that of the US Army in 1922, in compliance with legislation providing seven pay grades for both of the services. These were:

1st grade	Sergeant major, quartermaster sergeant	$74 per month
2nd grade	First sergeant, gunnery sergeant	$53
3rd grade	Staff sergeant	$45
4th grade	Sergeant	$45
5th grade	Corporal	$37
6th grade	Private first class	$35
7th grade	Private, drummer, trumpeter	$21

Up to World War II, a number of technical ratings and specialties had been added as the Corps increased the complexity of its structure and mission. These included master technical sergeant, drum major, paymaster sergeant, technical sergeant, supply sergeant, platoon sergeant, chief cook, field cook, field music corporal, and field music (replacing drummer and trumpeter). In keeping with the core values of the service, qualifying on the rifle range as an expert (the major-general commandant in Fred's first enlistment had this rating) or sharpshooter garnered an additional $5 or $3 monthly pay.

Training for the new officers who volunteered for the Corps and its reserve component emphasized the same values, only in a gentlemanly manner that continued through the war. The exaggerated, posturing style of USMC officer training often depicted in Hollywood treatments emerged in the decade following the Korean War, for reasons more related to the Cold War and service cultural changes. On November 14, 1940, the 1st Officers Candidate Class formed at Quantico to prepare several hundred civilian college graduates to be new officers in the expanding Corps. The Corps put some of its finest officers and NCOs to work with them. The commanding officer of Marine Corps

Dozens of new officers filled the ranks of the tank battalions, including Robert M. Neiman, commissioned in 1941, here a captain at Jacques' Farm signaling in a publicity shot from the turret of his M4A2 tank. He wears the tanker jacket, armored force helmet, and Resistol goggles. At the end of the war, he commanded the 1st Tank Battalion as a major. (Author's collection)

Schools was Colonel Lemuel C. Shepherd. Major Gerald Thomas served as his executive officer and commanded the 1st Candidates class. These two became, in a very short number of years, living icons of the Pacific war and postwar Marine Corps. The candidates mostly trained with sergeants, however, who proved strict and demanding, but fair. The instructors at OCC tended to be mostly senior men, gunnery sergeants experienced from the Banana Wars. The Corps combed worldwide for instructors, to make this experimental program work.

As the candidates finished the course and took the oath of office, they reported to the 4th Reserve Officer Course (ROC), as new second lieutenants. There they all fell under the charge, one might say the spell, of yet another Marine Corps icon, Major Merrill Twining. Twining was one of the most brilliant officers ever to have served in the USMC. One anecdote shows Twining's approach. One day, the lieutenants hiked the 20 miles to Manassas in full packs, listened to their briefings, walked the ground and learned the use of terrain in military tactics and maneuver. But then it began to rain right at mealtime. Twining remained out in the rain, sitting on a fence, chewing on a piece of grass, while they lined up outside and went through the service line in the one shelter set up for the meal. Nothing was said, but that demonstration illustrated, beyond all the lectures the second lieutenants had attended, how in the Marine Corps the officer looks to his troops before himself. Twining's words stuck with them: "Take care of your people and they will take care of you."

TRAINING

The first conventional, turreted, light tanks taken in USMC service were these M2A4s still painted in army olive drab, lined up at Camp New River in late 1941 in the 1st Tank Battalion park. Numbered T11–T28, they would see action on Guadalcanal, the only combat seen by that type tank. (USMC photo)

Marines like Fred Crowley who joined the first tank companies of the prewar and early World War II period had no benefit of school training, although officers frequently attended the US Army tank courses held at Fort Benning and Fort Knox from 1941 onwards. The early Marmon-Herrington tanks had required only the simplest automotive knowledge, since they incorporated current truck and auto engines and drive trains, and the band track remained simple in concept and maintenance. But with the expansion of the FMF, tanks began to arrive from the US Army

at a frantic rate. These were new production tanks of the M2A4 and M3 designs, which were used to fill out the first two tank battalions formed in late 1941. With the entry of the US into the war, the pace became more frenetic.

Harried army quartermasters had shipped several different configurations of M3 light tanks to the Marine Corps. One frustrated battalion commander wrote to headquarters: "At present, the Marine Corps seems to have the following types of tanks in the Pacific, several types of which belong to one unit [see plate B]: M2A4 gasoline, M3 gasoline hightop [cupola], M3 diesel hightop, modernized engine, M3 diesel hightop, engines not modernized, M3 hybrids, diesel and probably gas. Soon additional types will be added: M3A1, M3A3, M5 gas and diesel." These tanks arrived by the dozens at New River (later Camp Lejeune), North Carolina, and Camp Elliott, California, training bases with no operator's manuals or "nomenclature lists" (parts and components lists) that would give the troops at least some idea of how the tools and tanks were handled. Soon after his arrival, Fred and other enlisted men stood by while the officers and NCOs with some previous experience clambered on these mechanical novelties, started them and gingerly drove them off the railroad flatcars.

A mechanic adjusts the Continental W-670 radial engine of one of the M2A4 tanks of the headquarters section, A Company, 1st Tank Battalion. The early tanks used aircraft type radials, furnishing good power, but accounting for the height characteristic of US tanks. (USMC photo)

Captain Alexander Swencesky wrote directly to the quartermaster of the Marine Corps on November 12, 1941, requesting blueprints and standard nomenclature listings for the M3 tank and blueprints and operator's manuals for the W670 gasoline engine. He lamented, "at present, this organization [B Co., 2d Tk. Bn.] possesses no spare parts and has no suitable reference from which to order same."

Fortunately for Fred Crowley, he fell in with the older A Company, which had operated its M2A4 tanks since the end of 1940. Commanded

M2A4 tanks of A Company, 2d Tank Battalion, parade in Iceland. The tank commanders wear the older tank helmet used by the army infantry branch. The tanks never returned to the United States, and the tankers transferred to the south Pacific in 1942. (USMC photo)

ABOVE LEFT

While A Company guarded Iceland, tankers of B Company, 2d Tank Battalion, unloaded their M3 tanks at Tutuila, Pago Pago, American Samoa, and the first overseas deployment of the war began. Note the use of fiber sun helmets with standard utilities. The tank has its turret traversed to the rear, thus showing two stars. (USMC photo)

ABOVE RIGHT

An M3 light tank of B Company, 2d Tank Battalion, maneuvers at Camp Elliott. The tank commander wears the modern armor helmet and Resistol goggles. The fixed sponson machine guns, operated by the driver, are easily noted. Driver vision, once the hatches were closed, was limited to viewer slits and crude periscope devices. (USMC photo)

by Major Jesse Cook, the company was bound for Iceland with the 6th Marine Regiment (regiments of infantry, artillery and engineers are known as "nth Marines" in Marine Corps jargon) as the 1st Provisional Marine Brigade. In short order, Fred was shown how to field strip and clean the .30 caliber machine guns and how to traverse and point the 37mm gun in the turret, which few of the men had ever fired. As one of the newest to join, Fred would work for Sergeant Gearl M. "GM" English in 2d Platoon, breaking in as the assistant driver. But he had little time for driving practice as the company began to load the ships. His main job seemed to be the upkeep of the machine guns, one of which he operated in his position in the right front of the tank, and in maintaining the track and suspension system. The hurried pace of deployment permitted little time for tankers going across the sea. The men of their sister B Company, sent to Samoa in January 1942 as part of the defense forces there, had to fire their 37mm guns into an earthen bank on the way to the port of San Diego, to obtain their first experience operating the main gun of the light tanks.

Tank school

Only after the first two tank battalions had been shipped to the Pacific did the Marine Corps get around to forming a tank school for the training of crewmen and leaders for the five more battalions and separate tank units that would follow them. Headquarters detailed newly promoted Major William R. Collins, fresh from sea duty, to set up the Tank School, FMF Training Center, Camp Elliott. Starting in July 1942, he and his instructor staff would train marines to operate and maintain the various tanks and variants. Camp Elliott had already expanded with the purchase of more land for training, and Collins and the tankers of the battalions forming at Camp Elliott worked to build a camp and training facilities at "Jacques' Farm" at the same time that they struggled to devise a training program for the new vehicles and weapons. "Rip" Collins, who had attended the Fort Benning army tank officer course and operated the Marmon-Herringtons with 1st Tank Company in 1939, led the Tank School through all stages of its evolution, retraining the school and students in each new vehicle and new tactical concept emerging from the war and assisting in the formation of each tank battalion forming at Jacques' Farm. He would later take command of the 5th Tank Battalion, the last battalion to form in the US, lead it into the Pacific war and become the first active-duty general from the ranks of the World War II tank unit commanders.

Once the tyro tankers had finished the task of building their new school, they set to work organizing classes in tank nomenclature, driving, gunnery, tactical movement, maintenance, communications, and a host of related activities. Starting the second year of the war, cadre personnel arrived from the southwest Pacific, where tanks had first entered action in the Solomons. With news of the type of fighting in which USMC tankers had participated, classes could be organized to deal with the close assaults of Japanese infantry, the problems of antitank guns concealed in jungle foliage and problems of cooperation with the infantry, with whom no tactical drills had yet been devised. So enduring were some of these improvisations that sacks of flour were still being used to simulate close assault demolitions at the school three decades later, when the author was in training (see plate C).

The formation of the Tank School at least solved the problem of other FMF units dumping their misfits onto the new units as the divisions formed in late 1941. Although this phenomenon can be exaggerated, more than a few men like Fred were sent from the older units as most easily "spared" for detachment. The personnel reception center at the FMF Training Center, San Diego Area, now assigned

USMC Tank Units, 1923–46

1923–41
Light Tank Platoon, Marine Corps Expeditionary Force (1923–28)
1st Tank Company, 1st Marine Brigade (1937–41) → 1st Scout Company, 1st Marine Division
3d Tank Company, 1st Marine Brigade (1940–41) → A Co., 1st Tank Bn.
4th Tank Company, 2d Marine Brigade (1940–41) → A Co., 2d Tank Bn.
1st–2d Tank Battalions (1941)

1941–45
1st Scout Co., 1st Marine Division (1941–44)*
2d Scout Co., 2d Marine Division (1941–44)*
1st–6th Tank Battalions (1941–45)
1st–5th, 8th–11th Amphibian Tractor Battalions (1942–45)
1st Corps Medium Tank Battalion (1943–44)
1st Separate Tank Company (1942–43) → C Co., 3d Tank Bn.
2d Separate Tank Company (1942–44) → B Co., 6th Tank Bn.

1946
1st–2d Tank Battalions
10th–11th Tank Battalions, USMCR

* The divisional scout companies became dismounted units in 1943.

An M3A1 of B Company, 3d Tank Battalion, on the jungle trails of Bougainville, November 1943. Notice the pistol port open on the turret rear, for ventilation. Towing cables are ready for hookup to other tanks as bogging was frequent in such terrain. The antiaircraft machine gun is dismounted and could rarely be used in such close conditions. (US Army Signal Corps (SC) photo)

An M3A1 of 1st Tank Battalion parades in Australia, April 1943, where the division refitted after Guadalcanal. The sponson machine guns had disappeared with this model, but the tight fit for a crew of four remains evident. (USMC photo)

marines fresh out of basic training to tank and other specialty training from a broad pool. Occasionally, the whims of wartime brought unusual results, as on one day in 1943, when all newly arrived marines with last names beginning with A through C went to the tank course.

There does not seem to have been any such "dumping" done with officers, and many well-qualified ones, products of the National Emergency expansion program of 1940, as well as more than a few old China hands, came into leadership positions in the fledgling tank arm. From 1943 onward, the Tank School hummed with activity, as the M3 lights gave way to the new twin-engine M5s, and then came the first mediums, a set of 22 M4A4 tanks with the strange five-block Chrysler A57 engine. These proved a false start, though, as hundreds of M4A2 twin-diesel mediums arrived at Marine Corps depots a few months later and the lessons had to be rewritten again. There were no tactics manuals, just a few technical manuals and nomenclature lists for the vehicles. According to one seasoned instructor:

I never saw any training films at Jacques' Farm, except for maintenance films. We drew up our own training plans and organized each lesson as we saw fit within the plan, emphasizing practical application whenever possible. We did have the help of several factory representatives, primarily teaching the maintenance men, and these were some great guys. They provided a lot of local knowledge for us whenever we needed them.

Trainees became used to looking at the world through periscopes, and by mid-1944, the new tanks had vision rings around the commander's cupola, which improved conditions greatly. Being buttoned up in a tank, for somebody new, is a strange experience. Only the driver or tank commander can see very much and for some people it remains disorienting; many cannot endure it. Tank School operations officer Robert Neiman discovered that on average 10 percent of each training group would get claustrophobia when buttoned up:

GM English (my head driving instructor) and I figured this out at Jacques' Farm. English said to me, 'You know captain, we're wasting a lot of time trying to train these guys.' So we decided the first day we'd give every man a ride in a buttoned up tank, and just as we had calculated, one in 10 would throw up and we'd send him back the next day to the replacement camp at Camp Elliott, instead of wasting our time trying to make tankers out of them. The people who remained felt more or less at home. Regardless of how skilled we became though, the vision was very poor in the older light tanks, the M3s.

Tanks in USMC service

M1917 6-ton (acquired 1923)

Crew: 2

Weight: 13,400lb(unloaded)

Armor: .6in. (15mm) max, hull and turret

Armament: 37mm M1916 gun or .30 cal. MG

Engine: Buda HU 4-cyl. 42hp

Speed: 5.5mph

Range: 30 miles

Misc: Three acquired on loan from the army for amphibious exercises in the Caribbean, growing eventually to nine such machines in the light tank platoon, Marine Corps Expeditionary Force formed at Quantico. Five deployed to China with the platoon in 1927–28. Discarded in 1935.

Marmon-Herrington CTL-3 (1936)

Crew: 2

Weight: 9,500lb. (10,900lb. for CTL-3A)

Armor: 1/4in.

Armament: 3 .30 cal. MG

Engine: Lincoln V-12 110hp, Hercules 6 cyl. 124hp in CTL-3A

Speed: 33mph

Range: 125 miles

Misc: Turretless tank; prototype fitted with one .50 and two .30 cal. MG; band track. Five built; five more CTL-3A delivered in 1939 with 10.5in. track and reinforced suspension. The CTL-3s were rebuilt in 1941 as CTL-3A; all then redesignated CTL-3M. Equipped 1st Tank Company, FMF, later the tank platoons of 1st and 2d Scout Companies. All discarded in 1943.

M2A4 Light tank (1940)

Crew: 4

Weight: 23,500lb.

Armor: 1in. max. hull and turret

Armament: 1 37mm M5 and 1 .30 cal. MG in turret; 1 .30 cal. AA on turret; 3 .30 MG in hull.

Engine: Continental W-670 radial, 262hp

Speed: 36mph

Range: 70 miles

Misc: 36 acquired from US Army in 1940 as it became apparent that Marmon-Herrington designs could not be delivered in time. Equipped 3d and 4th Tank Companies, FMF, which became A Companies, 1st and 2d Tank Battalions in 1941. First 18 saw action at Guadalcanal with A Company, 1st Tank Battalion, the only combat employment of the M2A4. Discarded in 1943.

Marmon-Herrington CTL-6 (1941)

Crew: 2

Weight: 12,500lb. designed, 14,370lb. actual

Armor: 1/4in.

Armament: 3 .30 cal. MG

Engine: Hercules 6 cyl. 124hp

Speed: 33mph

Range: 125 miles

Misc: Turretless tank; improved version of CTL-3, with improved track and suspension components. Only 20 built, discarded in 1943 on Samoa.

Marmon-Herrington CTM-3TBD (1941)

Crew: 3

Weight: 18,500lb. designed, 21,180lb. actual

Armor: 1/2in.

Armament: 2 .50 cal. in turret, 3 .30 cal. MG in front hull

Engine: Hercules DXRB diesel, 123hp

Speed: 30mph

Range: 125 miles

Misc: Turreted version of CTL series tank; with improved track and suspension components. Only five built, discarded in 1943 on Samoa.

M3 Series Light tank (1941)

Crew: 4

Weight: 25,600lb. (26,000lb. for M3A1)

Armor: 1.5in. front 1.0in. side hull; 2.0in. gunshield (1.5 first production), 1.5in. front, 1.25in. side turret

Armament: 1 37mm M6 and 1 .30 cal. MG in turret; 1 .30 cal. AA on turret; 3 .30 MG in hull (1 in M3A1)

Engine: Continental W-670 radial, 262hp; some fitted with Guiberson T-1020 9 cyl. radial diesel, 245hp

Speed: 36 mph

Range: 70 miles (90 miles diesel)

Misc: Standard tank in USMC tank battalions through end of 1943. Used for flame-thrower 'Satan' tank 1943–44 as well. M3 introduces vertical gyrostabilizer for gun mount, M3A1 and later US World War II tanks fitted with power turret.

M5A1 Light tank (1943)

Crew: 4

Weight: 30,800lb.

Armor: 1.75in. lower front, 1.0in. side hull; 2.0in. gunshield, 1.5in. front, 1.25in. side turret

Armament: 1 37mm M6 and 1 .30 cal. MG in turret; 1 .30 cal. AA on turret; 1 .30 MG hull

Engine: Twin Cadillac V-8, 296hp

Speed: 36mph

Range: 100 miles

Misc: Issued to USMC tank battalions beginning in late 1943 (summer 1943 for 1st Tank Battalion from army stocks). In action in Cape Gloucester and Roi-Namur battles, a few remain at Saipan. Discarded late 1944.

M4A2 Medium Tank (1943)

Crew: 5

Weight: 66,000lb.

Armor: 2–4.25in. lower front, 2.5in. upper front, 1.5in. side hull; 3.5in. gunshield, 3.0in. front, 2.0in. side turret

Armament: 1 75mm M3 and 1 .30 cal. MG in turret; 1 .50 cal. AA on turret; 1 .30 MG hull

Engine: Twin GM diesels, 12-cyl. 410hp

Speed: 25mph

Range: 150 miles

Misc: Issued to 1st Corps Medium Tank Battalion in 1943, partial issue to all USMC tank battalions beginning in late 1943 (M4A1 with R-975 gas engine in summer 1943 for 1st Tank Battalion from army stocks). All USMC tank units convert during 1944. USMC is sole US user of diesel M4 tanks.

M4A3 Medium Tank (1944)

Crew: 5

Weight: 66,400lb.

Armor: 2–4.25in. lower front, 2.5in. upper front, 1.5in. side hull; 3.6in. gunshield, 3.0in. front, 2.0in. side turret

Armament: 1 75mm M3 and 1 .30 cal. MG in turret; 1 .50 cal. AA on turret; 1 .30 MG hull; 2in. mortar M3 (smoke) in turret

Engine: Ford GAA V-8, 500hp

Speed: 26mph

Range: 130 miles

Misc: Issued to USMC tank battalions beginning in late 1944. All USMC tank units convert during 1945, 1st Tank Battalion last. Postwar model is M4A3 with 105mm howitzer M4. Bulldozer and flame-thrower variants continue in USMC service until 1959.

Notes:

All weights are empty unless otherwise indicated

Armor figures are maximums

After tank school

Once familiarized with the tanks and trained to drive and shoot, the new tankers went to the various units forming in the San Diego and Camp Lejeune areas. Tank companies frequently formed with infantry regiments for initial unit training and fitting out, before they would be brought together in a division and the tank companies fell under a new battalion headquarters and commander. Continuing expansion after 1942, to fill the six marine divisions eventually fielded, placed an additional burden on the early battalions to provide cadres. For instance, the 2d Tank Battalion effectively divided in two, after a year's service, to create the 3d Tank Battalion, with both battalions then forced to accept new infusions of inexperienced men. The three tank battalions formed by late 1942 also took charge of the training and maintenance of the separate tank platoons of any nearby defense battalion, which sorely lacked the necessary parts and tool sets for tank maintenance.

Tank company commanders took most of the responsibility for training their units, and honing the teamwork required in tank crews and platoons. As time permitted, they also began to train with the infantry regiments. This last process did not begin to happen until late 1943 in the case of the 4th Marine Division and the two divisions that followed. Tank–infantry training had been nonexistent before 1943, and it showed at Guadalcanal and other actions. The bloody fighting at Tarawa alerted the 4th Marine Division to the dangers, and serious training and drilling between tank and infantry units followed. Mostly, though, it was a case of battle experience and improvisation that resulted in effective tank–infantry cooperation, and each division developed its standing procedures independently. A USMC doctrinal manual did not emerge until the fighting had ceased in the Pacific war. In the 4th Marine Division, an attempt was made to train tanks to drive through a friendly artillery barrage, set for airbursts, in the hope of reaching a new level of cooperation in arms. The C Company commander in the tank battalion (Neiman) recalled:

It sounded like rain on a tent as we took our M5s through the impact area. Everything went well, but I did have one casualty –

Infantrymen watch USMC tanks of 2d Tank Battalion on Tinian in a photo setting corresponding to later training standards of the war. The powerful M4A2 mediums lead a light tank, M5A1, and the early flame-thrower tank, a converted M3A1 called the "Satan." The tactical co-ordination of infantry and tanks emerged after much trial and error in the Pacific war. (US Navy (USN) photo)

2d Lt. Dick Pierson, from A Company, got in a tank to ride as the asst driver, and one of the periscopes was missing. The covers were just sheet metal weather caps and a fragment came right through, giving him a severe wound in the thigh. Although the 4th Marine Division worked hard training tank companies with the infantry battalions, it never managed to pull off a tank attack through its own artillery in combat.

A crewman acts as a ground guide while the driver backs this M2A4 tank on to a 45ft tank lighter in Iceland. The tanker wears the infantry-type prewar crash helmet, with its distinctive doughnut-shape padding, and the prewar blue denim coverall. (USMC photo)

APPEARANCE AND DRESS

Prewar uniforms

Fred wore the same uniforms and equipment his NCOs had worn when they patrolled in Central America or the Caribbean islands, issued in this case since 1927. The summer service uniform in khaki cotton or the worsted wool winter service green uniform that was worn everyday, according to the season, also became the field and combat uniform, by the addition of regulation field equipment – web gear, leggings, and helmet – of the current issue. There had been attempts to field a special uniform for dirty work details and field exercises since the 1920s, such as a blue denim uniform similar to the one used by the army, in both coverall and two-piece form, or navy dungarees. In 1940, the Corps adopted an official work/fatigue uniform, not yet intended for combat, called the "utility uniform." Approved on November 10, 1941, it was made of herringbone twill (HBT) cotton, a stiff, sturdy material much used at the time for civilian work clothing. In contrast to the army's olive drab, the Corps chose a similar yet distinctive sage-green material with a striking alternating diagonal weave, or chevron pattern, for most of its uniforms. Army olive drab HBT clothing occasionally had to be issued during periods of shortage, and in the case of specialty clothing.

Therefore when Fred sailed to Iceland in November 1940 with A Company, 2d Tank Battalion, and the 6th Marines, he wore the green wool winter service uniform. When in the field or on parade, he simply added leggings, helmet, web gear, pack, weapon, and associated equipment depending on the personal weapon he carried. A similar

overseas garrison mission, although not clear at the time, was performed by the battalion's B Company, when it shipped out to garrison Samoa with the 2d Brigade a month after Pearl Harbor. There the tankers wore their cotton khaki uniforms and even added fiber sun helmets as they worked on their tanks in the harsh tropical sun.

Marines of the 1st Separate Tank Company check their tanks after unloading them in September 1942 at Tutuila, American Samoa. They wear the summer service khaki uniforms and garrison caps, some with fiber sun helmets. One man wears the early prewar coverall. The center tank is the Marmon-Herrington CTL-6 tankette. All 20 of these saw their sole use with the two separate tank companies guarding Samoa. Behind it are the rare CTM-3TBD turreted Marmon-Herringtons. (USMC photo)

New uniforms for the Pacific war

After the war started, an avalanche of new uniforms and equipment descended on the marines in their bases and camps, in the same chaotic way that all the different types of tanks had come in at the railheads. The P1941 HBT utility uniform began the new "look" for World War II. Its shirt, or jacket in USMC nomenclature, had two large patch pockets on the front skirt and a smaller one on the left breast. The Marine Corps eagle-globe-anchor emblem was stenciled, topped with "USMC," all in black ink, on the breast pocket. Four metal-plated buttons fastened the front, with two more closing the cuffs, on each sleeve. The P1941 HBT trousers proved equally conventional, with two slash pockets in front (some manufacturers added a small watch pocket), two patch pockets on the rear, a fly secured by four or five buttons, and belt loops for the service web belt. A cap, called a "cover" in naval parlance, completed the uniform, at first borrowed from the army design, but it was replaced in 1944 by a new design. The new shape has survived to the present day, although postwar starching and blocking converted it into a more serious piece of head gear.

Second Lieutenant Joseph Dever and some of his crewmen of the 1st Corps Medium Tank Battalion display several uniform items in this posed shot, probably taken at New Caledonia. In late 1943, all have the standard armor force helmet, Resistol goggles and wear the P1941 HBT utility. The submachine guns are all Thompson .45 caliber M1A1. Dever would fight later on Iwo with 4th Tank Battalion and earn a silver star. (USMC photo)

The P1944 HBT utility uniform appeared later in the war, fitted with deep cargo pockets on the trouser sides and (on some variants) rear, and internal front pockets on the jacket, all intended to increase integral carrying capacity for troops operating in combat without packs and web gear. These saw first use at Iwo Jima and continued in service well after the Korean War. The marines disliked the stiffness of the initial issue HBT dungarees, and used to wash them repeatedly, or even drag them on lines over the sides of their ships. This not only softened the uniforms, but also gave them a more desired veteran-like or "salty" appearance.

Camouflage uniforms first drawn from army stocks, the M1942 one-piece (and an earlier one-piece known derisively as the "frog suit"), were initially used only by the Marine Corps raider battalions, but gained acceptance for general Marine Corps use in mid-1942. The marines applied the usual USMC and insignia stencils on the USMC P1942 reversible camouflage uniform breast pocket as well as its successor, the P1944 reversible camouflage uniform. Camouflage helmet covers were issued for use with these and the standard utility uniform, and much mixing occurred in the field, as uniforms wore out or replacements were received under varied conditions. The camouflage uniforms in any case remained scarce and never matched the numbers of marines engaged on any campaign. With the issue of green and camouflage HBT utilities, the normal white underwear or "skivvy" shirt became a handicap to proper camouflage in the field, and a green tee-shirt came into issue. The camouflage reversible helmet cover, however, became a significant USMC item in late 1942, appearing in several different patterns, and remained a standard issue item and a signature of the Marine Corps forever after. The reversible color tones alternated between green and brown motifs, leading to the phrase, "green side out, brown side out, run in circles, scream and shout," as a satirical view of Marine Corps routine, with its (implicitly) constantly changing orders.

New footwear replaced the World War I leather field shoe with its steel horseshoe-insert heel. This time there was a more practical rubber sole and heel and better waterproofing. These boots gained fame as the famous USMC "boondocker" after its acceptance in 1941. The thick, rough-side-out, brown suede leather of the boondocker contrasts with the smooth black finish, spit 'n' polish look of the field boots used over a decade later. The P1936 field legging was another Marine Corps-specific item, lighter in color and slightly shorter than the army item. The leggings fell into haphazard use rapidly in Pacific theater combat, but remained an issue item until after the Korean War.

A posed publicity shot taken in April 1944 at 2d Tank Battalion of the crew of the B Company commander's tank, B40 "Betio," shows the standard tanker uniforms, eschewing the leggings of the infantrymen and wearing the standard boondocker boot. (USMC photo)

The World War I M1917A1 helmet saw use in the first combat actions of the Corps at Wake Island, the Philippines, and in the early island garrisons. But by the middle of 1942 it had been almost completely supplanted by the familiar M1 helmet used by all the US services for the rest of the war and nearly the rest of the century.

Marine Corps identification tags varied in composition and content, but essentially remained the 1917 navy-style oval, with one or two holes, hung on a variety of chains, cords, wire, and cloth tape. The usual information stamped on the tags included the marine's name, service number, date of birth, "USMC," blood type (starting 1941) and, until 1942, an acid-etched fingerprint.

The basic issue "782 gear" drawn by Marine Corps tankers was the same as all other field marines but saw more limited use by them. Tankers like Fred usually formed up with field marching packs for boarding ships and then threw their gear either in the vehicles or into company storage when the time came to make a landing. Going ashore, Fred carried his pistol in a hip or shoulder holster, with the magazine pouches clipped to the web belt. In the tank, he stowed his steel helmet, pistol belt, with more magazine pouches, a canteen and cup in its carrier, and the first-aid kit. Hardtack rations, mess kits, extra ammunition, submachine guns and magazines, knives, entrenching tools and their carriers, rain ponchos and tent shelter halves all disappeared into the nooks and crannies of the tank. The officers added binoculars and map cases. With a full load of ammunition for the tank weapons, there would be little room to spare for the crewmen, and the tight spaces and even narrower hatches meant that very little equipment could be carried on their bodies.

A few tank-specific items finished off their usual garb. Most prominent was the standard "football"-type crash or tank helmet. An army creation, it had been developed in various forms in the 1930s. The version Fred usually wore in 1941, and throughout the war, was the Tank Helmet, developed for the mechanized cavalry, with its hard plate flaps hinged to permit the radio-intercom headset to be worn and used. Another version, the Infantry Tank Helmet, had soft leather earflaps and soft cups for the headset. Both types at first incorporated an external "doughnut" ring of padding around the entire helmet, and the cavalry helmet was the version accepted when the tanks of the infantry and the mechanized cavalry were combined in the army's Armored Force of 1940. Shortly afterwards, the doughnut padding was abandoned (nobody knows why). The final M1942 Armored Forces helmet went into mass production by Rawlings, but the earlier types remained in use in the US and Fred wore one of these when he went to Iceland with his company. Sometimes the cloth winter helmet lining would be worn alone, as it was cheaper and more comfortable in training. Topping off the helmet was a set of protective goggles, at first the Resistol M1938 patented by the Harry Buegueliesen Company, with tempered lenses in steel frames. In wartime, a simpler, one-piece plastic lens came into use, finally standardized as the M1944 goggles, foam-lined and issued in a tough box with two tinted spare lenses. These last remain in service among present-day US forces.

The intercom and radio communications used by tankers was an Army Signal Corps HS-23 headset with two R-14 earpiece receivers, connected with a S-141 toggle switch to the T-30 throat induction microphone or the T-17 hand microphone. These connected to the radio-intercom system, which by 1943 was the army standard Signal Corps SCR-508A and 528A radio. What Fred first used, though, in his M2A4 was a navy radio set, since the Marine Corps had equipped his M2A4 and other early tanks (through 1943) with aircraft radios, the ubiquitous model GF/RU.

Next came the coverall, a prized uniform item, called the "working suit, one-piece," made from army HBT material and available since 1938 for mechanics, paratroopers, tankers, and airmen.

This pose by an M3 crew of 2d Tank Battalion uncharacteristically shows all wearing the early-type coverall, perhaps available to many tankers in 1942, when only six tank companies existed in the Corps. In the hot and wet climate of the southwest Pacific, where they saw their first combat, the coveralls would have been too uncomfortable in any case. (USMC photo)

These were issued to units, not individuals. Only the arcane workings of the supply system, aided by dumb luck, brought these into the hands of tank crewmen, and not just mechanics. An improved "late" version, released in 1943, had a darker, more olive color, and featured larger hip pockets and closing flaps, with a single-breast pocket, instead of the two placed on the predecessor suit. The usual USMC and emblem was stenciled on the left breast pocket.

Topping off the tanker ensemble was the ever-popular winter jacket, combat (the "tanker's jacket"), made of cotton twill with a heavy wool liner, and fitted with knitted cuffs, collar, and waistband to keep out the wind and dust from road marches. Because of the typically erratic and slow supply flow in the Pacific theater, the usual isolation of Marine Corps units (except those refitting in Hawaii), and the adverse effects of tropical climates upon clothing, tankers would wear all kinds of clothing articles. Parts of camouflage, P1942 or P1944 HBT dungarees, P1941 field jackets, tanker jackets, and coveralls might be worn by a single person and mixed among marines of the same platoons.

Tank crew garb in combat

Once away from the garrison "flagpole," where formations, inspections, and parades required strict rules on the proper wearing of uniforms and equipment, the variations made by enlisted men and officers alike challenged the imaginations of the most seasoned veterans. Tank units frequently operated independently, supporting the assigned infantry units but not administratively attached to them. Thus, platoons and companies out of sight of battalion commanders and meddlesome staff officers could relax into a state of undress, especially when in a hot and humid tropical setting. Leggings disappeared first, by most accounts, and then shirts disappeared entirely. The majority of men wore no underwear, to fend off heat rash. Photos frequently show bare-chested

marines laboring or relaxing on atolls freshly conquered from the Japanese, growing mustaches (but not beards) and long hair, but not neglecting their weapons or machines in the least.

As temperatures soared and battles raged across coral atolls and larger islands crowded with jungles or sprawling cane fields, the tankers had no respite, as they had to fight "buttoned up" to guard against the Japanese infantry, some suicidal, who would swarm over any tank with open hatches. When they emerged in rear areas to rearm, refuel, and perform needed maintenance, they would work in tee-shirts, often leaving their personal weapons still in the tanks in their haste to work and return to action. Then they would put their headsets and helmets back on, don jackets or coveralls and their weapons, and roll back to the front lines. At night, they would gather behind the infantry lines in laagers, unless they were needed up front to help repel an attack. There they would rest and sleep alongside or underneath their tanks, rolling up in shelter halves or a blanket (Iwo Jima was cold and not tropical in February) and keeping their pistols, grenades, Thompson submachine guns, or a dismounted Browning .30 caliber machine gun at the ready to deal with infiltrators or breakthroughs. The contrasts in appearance of marines alternately in action or in the rear made for many surreal scenes in the midst of the toughest island campaigns.

The jocular pose of the tank company commander (compare with the shot on page nine) and executive officer on board ship after their first combat in early 1944 shows the casual way the P1941 HBT utility uniform could be worn, with boondocker boots or shower shoes as footwear. Note the typical oval-shaped identification tags. (USN photo)

BELIEF AND BELONGING

By the time Fred and his brother marines left the United States and entered combat, the *esprit de corps* of the USMC had been refined and decided for all time. The Marine Corps instilled discipline and cohesion in basic training, and the peculiar Marine Corps culture provided a continuing bond even with the transfers made necessary by wartime expansion, detachment, and attachment to other units. Unit commanders and non-coms came and went, but the loyalty to one's buddies and platoons common to all fighting men remained, becoming inflated in a Marine Corps setting that made one willing to fight in any circumstance to defend the honor of the Corps at large. In particular, marines carried the twin desires to take revenge not only for Pearl Harbor, but also for Wake Island, the epic defense of a lonely atoll by a few hundred marines of the 1st Defense Battalion, who had taken Japanese ships, planes, and hundreds of soldiers down in their last stand against overwhelming odds. As the Pacific war continued, the first year of experiences at Guadalcanal, the other Solomons Islands, and Tarawa confirmed in the minds and souls of these soldiers of the sea that the Japanese were not supermen, but that they would fight to the last man. Moreover, the Japanese offered and received no quarter in their fight, killing Americans who tried to save their wounded and offer an easy surrender.

This unique spirit was engendered at basic training level. Recruits were presented with a grueling, unrelenting series of training days, each lasting from 0400 to 2200, filled with physical exercise, the pressure of task after task, close supervision by drill sergeants, myriad combat drills, and general military training. At the end of that period – usually eight seemingly endless weeks – they paraded and received the compliments of their leaders, who called them "men" and "marines" for the first time since they entered the recruit training depot. From then on, the new marines walked as equals among legendary NCOs and officers who had fought with the Corps in a third of a century of wars and expeditions, from the Boxer Rebellion to the Banana Wars.

The veterans of the Old Corps still had a mighty role to play in the expanded Marine Corps of World War II. Although no veterans of tank actions existed in the prewar Corps, the steady hand of division commanders who had been sergeants at Belleau Wood in 1918, or gunnery sergeants and sergeants major who had fought in France and in the jungle patrolling Nicaragua and Haiti, left an indelible impression on the men and junior officers who joined after 1940. Like the legions of ancient Rome, or the Spanish *tercios* of the late Renaissance, the US Marines functioned as an elite military organization. Even after the December 1942 presidential decision ended all volunteering and converted US manpower to the Selective Service system – thereby forcing the Corps to accept draftees for the first time in its history – a system of persuasion and volunteering operated within Selective Service. Slightly more than 10 percent of marines serving in the course of the war were the only true inductees of the draft. The creed of the US marine spread easily over the 669,000 men and women who would serve before the Japanese surrender. "Once a marine, Always a marine," has for generations sufficed to describe the sense of patriotism, pride, discipline, loyalty, and brotherhood that has carried the Corps through perils and triumphs.

It comes as no surprise then, how Fred and his buddies greeted the coming of war. Off duty on a fine Sunday morning, they gathered by the bus stop to go into San Diego and take in a movie or play billiards. Some sat down for the first matinee and a civilian man went on stage and announced that Japan and the US were at war. After a moment of silence, they all threw their hats in the air and cheered, and began singing the Marine's Hymn. Fred was shaking with excitement. If the Japanese had seen the reaction they had prompted, what came next would have

M4A2 tanks of A Company, 1st Tank Battalion, form on the middle of the airfield at Peleliu, after the defeat of the ineffectual Japanese tank charge there. The unusual display of pennants on the radio antennae demonstrates how little Marine Corps tankers feared Japanese antitank guns at this point in the war, although track blocks are mounted on turret sides and hull front as extra protection. (USMC photo)

An M4A1 tank of A Company, 1st Tank Battalion, protects its infantry squad at Cape Gloucester in January 1944. This was the only use of the M4A1 model tank, issued to the company by the US Army from stocks available in Australia for the operation. (USMC photo)

bothered them even more. Called into formation that afternoon at Camp Elliott, their company commander gave a stirring pep talk. At the end he exclaimed, "By God, if we have to go to war, there's no one we'd rather fight!" The tankers cheered wildly.

In such an environment, the thought of failure or letting down one's brother marines remained unthinkable and, on the contrary, inspired legendary feats of exertion and courage. One of Fred's platoon sergeants, Bob McCard, became a gunnery sergeant in A Company for the Saipan landing in mid-1944. His citation for the Medal of Honor speaks volumes:

For conspicuous gallantry and intrepidity at the risk of his life above and beyond the call of duty while serving as Platoon Sergeant of Company A, Fourth Tank Battalion, Fourth Marine Division, during the battle for enemy Japanese-held Saipan, Mariana Islands, on June 16, 1944. Cut off from the other units of his platoon when his tank was put out of action by a battery of enemy 77-mm. guns, Gunnery Sergeant McCard carried on resolutely, bringing all the tank's weapons to bear on the enemy, until the severity of hostile fire caused him to order his crew out the escape hatch while he courageously exposed himself to enemy guns by hurling hand grenades, in order to cover the evacuation of his men. Seriously wounded during this action and with his supply of grenades exhausted, Gunnery Sergeant McCard dismantled one of the Tank's machine guns and faced the Japanese for the second time to deliver vigorous fire into positions, destroying sixteen of the enemy but sacrificing himself to insure the safety of his crew. His valiant fighting spirit and supreme loyalty in the face of almost certain death reflect the highest credit upon Gunnery Sergeant McCard and the United States Naval Service. He gallantly gave his life for his country.

ON CAMPAIGN

Early "tanking" in the Marine Corps

Camp Elliott, California, hummed with activity in May 1941, as Fred trudged from the 6th Marines area over to the tank park with his seabag slung over his shoulder. Camp Elliott, a mere 15 miles north of San Diego, occupied about 30,000 acres with its wartime annexations completed. It sported the usual "semi-permanent" wooden 50-man barracks (which had a true permanence in the Corps), fortunately provided with oil heaters for the winter chill. Nearby stood heads (latrines) with plumbing and mess halls, run by each battalion or regiment. Built in 1934 as Camp Holcomb for the west coast brigade of the new FMF, with machine-gun and artillery firing ranges, it was renamed Camp Elliott in 1940, the year Fred rejoined his regiment from sea duty. It was an ideal location, close enough to San Diego to take in a movie or enjoy a day in the park. On base, there was a camp movie house and a post exchange able to supply most personal needs. The training routine was very limited, as the artillery and infantry had priority for the ranges, and the tankers practiced driving and moving in formations much more than shooting. Fred would not fire the 37mm gun until he returned from his first overseas deployment.

On the east coast, though, things were far more primitive. The brigade base there was Quantico, Virginia, one of the oldest posts of the Corps, with multistoried brick barracks and administrative buildings. But Quantico already housed the Marine Corps Schools, depot activities, and maintenance facilities, and was too cramped for the 1st Marine Division. Raised from brigade status, it returned from training in Cuba to fill out its regiments at Parris Island before moving, in September 1941, into the newest camp in the Marine Corps, Camp New River, North Carolina. Located midway between the ports of Wilmington and Morehead City, with little sign of local life other than tenant farms, it was a camp in name only. Established on March 1, 1941, the Marine Barracks, New River, would grow to 85,000 acres in a year, but the facility then still under construction was known as Tent Camp. While there were "semi-permanent" mess halls, heads, and showers, and a few temporary warehouse buildings, the officers and men of the division lived under canvas tenting raised over wooden decks placed on the sandy soil. In August 1942, the base became Camp Lejeune and the new barracks and administrative buildings would support the wartime expansion units. But by that time, the 1st Marine Division was long gone to the southwest Pacific.

The tank park and tank training area, like Camp Elliott's, was set away from the main base, a couple of miles south of Tent Camp. It appeared to have been a cotton farm. The rather dilapidated farmhouse was pressed into service for maintenance and security personnel. The sole remaining residents of the farm were dozens of rattlesnakes. It was a bit daunting to have them slithering around, but those who survived the tanks' treads soon moved out. The newly designated 1st Tank Battalion stood up on November 1, 1941, and started driver training as rapidly as the new tanks were placed in service.

The "semi-permanent" barracks buildings of Camp Elliott, California, would be the best accommodations seen by US Marines in the war, except for those fortunate to garrison Samoa or reform in Australia and New Zealand. In any event, all would be distant memories by mid-1944. (USMC photo)

In early July 1941, Fred and the rest of A Company, 2d Tank Battalion, drove their 18 tanks to the navy piers at San Diego, where stevedores loaded them with cranes and slings into the transports assigned to carry them to Iceland, via the Panama Canal. This would be Fred's longest voyage in his brief service in the Marine Corps, far longer than his cruiser had steamed in his earlier sea duty experience. The 1st Provisional Marine Brigade sailed to garrison Iceland, relieving a British garrison, as part of President Roosevelt's policy to give all possible aid, short of war, to the embattled British, now alone in the war against Hitler's Germany and Mussolini's Italy. Only two platoons completed the trip, as one transport stopped at Charleston to embark scout cars and other needed items, and six tanks had to be left behind.

Once on Iceland, there really was not very much to do. The Icelandic women remained off-limits to the marines, and Camp Whitehorse, near the village of Aldufoss, offered few comforts, beyond the well-heated huts left behind by the Brits. There was little training, and most of the time was spent on stevedore working parties at the port. After the Japanese attack on Pearl Harbor, the transports returned to pick up the brigade, now sorely needed in the Pacific. The dozen M2A4 light tanks, over which Fred and his crewmen had sweated so much, were left in the hands of a US Army regiment that took over the garrison.

The Marine Corps tank

Thus far, the life of a tanker in the Marine Corps showed little in the way of distinction. The Corps had only 46 tanks in service when Fred joined A Company, divided equally between the two new marine divisions. Marines knew that they wanted tanks for their modern FMF organization, but so much was needed to forge a nascent amphibious force at the same time that an understandable hiatus ensued. No army tanks of any note had been built in the US between the wars, apart from a few test machines. There were hundreds of light and medium tanks left over from World War I in army hands and, eventually, the Corps had borrowed or leased nine M1917A1 light tanks, built from the French Renault FT-17 design, for use in testing tanks in the landing trials of the 1920s. Five of these had deployed to China to reinforce the 3d Brigade at Tientsin in 1927–28, but had been discarded upon their return.

At the end of 1933, the FMF replaced the old Marine Corps Expeditionary Force that had existed before World War I. Planning began for the organization, equipment and doctrine that would support a wartime force of 25,000 men, consisting chiefly of a brigade of all arms on each coast with companion air groups and specialized defense battalions. This new FMF included a tank company in each of the two brigades. The question remained, what tank would it be? The answer posed the first of many challenges that would shape but also daunt the tank arm of the Marine Corps. The Marine Corps budgeting for the FMF initially permitted only the Quantico-based 1st Brigade to be outfitted in the first three years, and the west coast 2d Brigade, based at San Diego, would remain with only an infantry regiment – the 6th Marines – on hand. For its sole tank company then, the Corps selected the Marmon-Herrington CTL-3, contracted at the end of 1935. This turretless, two-man tank employed the Lincoln V-12 engine and rubber band track over a quadruple bogie-wheel suspension to move at a maximum speed of 33mph. Equipped with dual driving controls, it carried three ball mounts in the hull front for the intended weapons. Predictably, the two crew members had difficulties handling three machine guns as well as their other crew duties. The lack of a turret left the vehicle vulnerable on the sides and rear. The company commander also noted that since the navy was able to lift the 21-ton tank lighter from the transport and place it in the sea, a heavier tank ought to be considered for landing force use, especially some of the newer light tanks then entering service with the army.

These and other criticisms of the CTL-3 tank scarcely interrupted the acquisitions plan, though, as the Corps had already contracted with the Marmon-Herrington Company for a second platoon of tanks (CTL-3A), delivered on June 16, 1939. The USMC formally activated the 1st Tank Company, 1st Marine Brigade, on March 1, 1937, although it remained in equipment and personnel a mere platoon for a considerable time. The company participated in the annual fleet exercises and in 1940 it would take both platoons of CTL-3 and 3A tanks as well as a single army light tank, the new M2A4. The beginning of the European war enhanced the seriousness but not the size of the January–February 1940 exercise, which served mostly to test newer navy landing craft. The M2A4 showed that it could operate from these landing craft quite well, although the suspension system proved vulnerable to saltwater, causing some consternation among the tankers. The newer model CTL-3A handled much better, proving that the Marmon-Herrington engineers could improve as well.

Events moved far too rapidly for normal peacetime planning, however. As the Battle of France ensued and the British Army retreated from the continent of Europe, the commandant general received a disturbing memo from his chief planner, Charles D. Barrett, a brigadier-general and the chief architect of the 1930s amphibious doctrine. Noting that the Corps had ten Marmon-Herrington tanks in hand, 20 more on order and a further five of the new turreted 9-tonners on order, Barrett asserted that more urgent measures were now necessary:

> Several factors have recently arisen which materially affect the policy of the Marine Corps with respect to tanks. First. The present war has demonstrated the great effectiveness of tanks, and the relative numbers of tanks to other arms has been greater than formerly thought desirable. Second … it seems probable that in a number of cases, that the FMF could land without opposition and would then be called upon to defend a relatively large area. In this event a fast striking force would constitute the best defense. Third. The possibility of being ordered on operations before new tanks can be built has been increased. In this case, Army tanks actually on hand would constitute the only supply.

On July 8, 1940, the Secretary of the Navy formally requested 36 army light tanks from the Secretary of the Army. As new regiments formed and the expansion of tank companies to battalions ensued, the old Marmon-Herrington tanks went to the division special troops with their newly designated scout companies, leaving the M2A4-equipped 3d and 4th

Tank Companies as cadre for the new battalions. Both 1st and 2d Scout Companies operated the Marmon-Herrington CTL-3 tank and the four-wheel M3A1 armored scout car. The commandant general ordered M3 tanks in March 1941 to complete the requirement for the first two tank battalions, which were to operate three companies of light tanks and a fourth of Marmon-Herringtons: the last with the new turretless CTL-6 and the new three-man turreted tank, called the CTM-3TBD, which had been ordered before the move to army procurement sources.

The tank park routine

As Fred and his pals operated their M2A4s in Iceland and the B Company tankers, with their M3s on Samoa in 1942, learned about tanks in the tropics, the stateside tankers in the USMC operated under much the same primitive circumstances. The first tanks in the prewar Corps had been delivered to Quantico, a well-established base with paved motor pool and artillery parks, ordnance and maintenance activities, and the nearby Marine Corps Schools and Marine Corps Equipment Board in support. But at Camp Lejeune and Camp Elliott, tankers found themselves literally put out in the sandlot, away from any dedicated infrastructure, and frequently they had to build their own maintenance facilities from materials at hand. Late in the war, the Camp Lejeune plant began to emerge amid feverish wartime construction, but the last tank units had formed there in early 1944, and would enjoy the newer facilities only after the war.

Camp Elliott's expansion included a parcel of farmland, known forever by the Marine Corps tankers as Jacques' Farm, where they constructed their tank park and later tank school. Each morning, they would fall out of their barracks, wash and have breakfast, hold formation and then march over a mile to the tank park. Then would begin the timeless, sometimes backbreaking, routine of tank maintenance. The

The Corps filled out its first three tank battalions with the M3 light tank, which was shipped in a baffling array of different models to novice tankers at the east and west coast bases. Many of these remained in their army issue olive drab color, but a distinctive USMC green paint slowly became standard beginning in 1942. (USMC photo)

track and bogie wheels required lubrication and adjustment, because the band track of the Marmon-Herrington, and the rubber-bushed "live" track blocks of the army-type light tanks worked best with specific track tensions and torque settings on critical bolts. The various engines had to be started daily and checked out, the most arduous being the radial diesel equipping some of the M3 series tanks. The Guiberson diesel, model T-1020-4, had no starter motor, but relied instead on a compressed gas starter, using explosive cartridges placed in a cylinder mounted against the engine firewall. But first, the engine had to be manually cranked to remove any oil pooling in the lower cylinder heads.

Turrets had no power until the M3A1 appeared at the end of 1941, which meant that little maintenance was required of the simple bell crank and gearing. A single 12-volt battery served the early light tanks, but the radios appeared to be a puzzle. Because of the rush to ship light tanks to the Marine Corps, army quartermasters rounded up all models of light tanks from various sources. Some tanks came fitted with the navy aircraft model GF/RU, while others had British Army No. 19 radio sets ordered as substitutes for the RU and some of these had instructions in Russian, so confused were the supply channels dealing with various Lend-Lease transfer programs.

After each operation, the tanks had to be washed, refueled, and shut down, and the dust and dirt brought in through the hatches or the shoes of the crew removed from the crew compartment. Dust filters had to be cleaned and any repairs written up for the maintenance section to handle. If machine guns had been taken to the field, these had to be cleaned – the early M2 and M3 light tanks carried five of these for a four-man crew to handle – and then the tankers had their personal weapons and gear to clean and turn in after the tank was parked and tarped. Ever since the tank was invented, the old rule of four hours of maintenance for every hour of operation has stood as an iron law, regardless of epoch or current technology.

Above all, the tankers worked with no manuals for maintenance and operation of the various tanks that arrived at short notice on rail flatcars to be unloaded at Camp New River and Camp Elliott. In the new 3d Tank Battalion of late 1942, the commanders telegrammed headquarters that the 100-hour check was not performed on their new M3A1 tanks due to lack of tool sets; the tanks were approaching the 200-hour operation point and they needed the tools urgently. The three tank battalions formed by late 1942 also took charge of the training and maintenance of the separate tank platoons formed for several of the defense battalions, perhaps a dozen, which sorely lacked the necessary parts and tool sets for tank maintenance, not to mention experienced personnel. For all the new tank battalions, enormous shortfalls still existed in trained personnel, tactical and maintenance publications, parts, and services, but the desired organizational structure had been achieved.

Each tank company was designed to operate independently from its battalion, supporting an infantry regiment that itself might be apart from the rest of the marine division. Thus, the tank company had its own mechanics (including a maintenance officer), truck drivers, cooks, and admin clerks. The battalion headquarters company included a maintenance platoon and a battalion maintenance officer, but the majority of services took place on the company tank ramp.

The flat-top problem

The army had decided to install power turret traverse in the M3 series and the turret "basket" already proven beneficial in British designs. The basket was a turret floor hung under the turret ring, permitting the turret occupants to remain seated with the gun and mount at all times. The use of welding would increase in this M3A1 design and a simple periscope replaced the commander's cupola. So far so good, but the army decided to modify the M3 production with some of these "improvements" while the retooling to M3A1 production took place simultaneously. This action resulted in the delivery of many M3 "hybrid" tanks at the end of the M3 production run, fitted with the new flat-top turret and gun mount but without power traverse and basket. But the mount designed for the missing power traverse also lacked the 20-degree gymbal movement formerly used by the gunner to lay on target, using shoulder yokes. The tank commander-loader handled the manual traverse but had no gunner's sight, while the gunner had elevation but no final traverse control. These M3 hybrid tanks, including the usual proportion fitted with diesel engines, were shipped to Marine Corps bases at the same time that the M3A1 production began to arrive, producing howls of protest from the already harassed tankers. Dubbed "flat-tops," the hybrids were condemned as unfit for combat and useless even for training. Apparently, similar tanks went to the British Army as part of scheduled Lend-Lease shipments. Their ordnance shops in the field changed the manual traverse to the gunner's position to solve the immediate problem, but the Corps lacked any such field capability in 1942.

To the 'ville

Tank training on the east coast came to an end in late 1943, after the formation of a company of 4th Tank Battalion and the last three defense battalion tank platoons. The Tank School continued to operate at Camp Elliott (Jacques' Farm), but the 4th and 5th Tank Battalions stood up at Camp Pendleton, California, a much larger tract purchased in 1942 by the Marine Corps for the training of the wartime expansion divisions. Southern California offered much more lively entertainment for the officers and enlisted men than the relatively poor and isolated coast of North Carolina. Time remained short, for the divisions deployed to the Pacific after only a few months of unit training. The 6th Marine Division and its 6th Tank Battalion actually formed from separate regiments and tank companies overseas, only one regiment and tank company forming at Pendleton in September 1944. Thereafter, only replacement training continued in the United States.

The average age of marines in a tank company forming at Camp Pendleton was 19 years. For these young men, southern California was filled with temptations of drink and of the flesh, available from Los Angeles to Tijuana. The coming of the war changed many attitudes in America, of course, and sexual mores began to loosen as well. There was more of an attitude of "here today, gone tomorrow." Men had been brought up with the notion that "nice girls" didn't do "that" until they got married and that most girls who would go to bed with you would not do so on the first date. But a marine had a steady persistence and would try to convince a girl that he was the kind of guy she wanted to have a sexual relationship with, even though convincing her might take quite a while. Later in New Zealand and Australia, marines of the 1st and 2d Marine Divisions found a new kind of girlfriend. In mid-1942, a civilian technical representative visiting Camp Pendleton remarked:

> During some of my recent travels on the west coast, I was privileged to spend some of my time in a camp with a newly organized Medium Tank Battalion. Both officers and men were a friendly crowd and made my stay very pleasant. As the battalion was preparing to break camp and leave for active service in a foreign theater, the men were winding up their affairs and having their last fling at social life before leaving.
>
> Living and working with the men over a period of 7 to 10 days impressed me with their lack of experience and training in mechanical work and the use of mechanized equipment. The officers were mostly young and fresh out of college, very eager to get into the fighting but in my opinion very much unprepared for it, being more interested in social activities and the sowing of a few wild oats. One of the most dangerous explosives known can be made from liquor and mechanized equipment and this situation should be avoided as much as possible. I was annoyed by the looseness of control and lack of authority exercised over the soldiers [sic] by the officers who were very seldom with the troops at all. A large number of the officers and men were on leave, which may have made the situation appear worse than it really was. These troops were about to go into battle with highly mechanized equipment but knew very little about its

maintenance, and although now equipped with brand new tanks, would soon be faced with preventative maintenance problems, which would require experienced direction.

The first two marine divisions shipped out for the south Pacific in the summer of 1942. The 3d Marine Division, which formed in September 1942, followed during January and February 1943. The 4th Marine Division formed in September 1943 and shipped out to participate in the Marshall Islands invasion from the west coast the following January. So, "here today, gone tomorrow" became a commonplace for most Marine Corps ground units of World War II. Yet the island campaigns proved to be bursts of combat, lasting from a single day to six weeks, for the most part. Marine divisions and their tank units thus spent most of the war deployed to island bases for training and regrouping after these battles, many of which proved epic in nature.

Into battle
The marine divisions sent overseas in 1942 were supposed to train in New Zealand as the I Marine Amphibious Corps and then begin the amphibious campaign in 1943 across the central Pacific. But the Japanese advance down the Solomon Islands chain proved too threatening, and the 1st Marine Division had to go into action much earlier than anticipated, landing at Guadalcanal and Tulagi Islands on June 7, 1942. With one of its infantry regiments, the 7th Marines, on occupation duty in Samoa, with its attached C Company, 1st Tank Battalion, the 2d Marines had to come from the west coast, with C Company, 2d Tank Battalion. Thus, the first Marine Corps tank fight came when a pair of M3A1 light tanks from C Company, 2d Tank Battalion, attacked on August 8, 1942 at Tanambogo (next to Tulagi) while its battalion still awaited shipping on the west coast with the rest of the 2d Marine Division.

Companies A and B, 1st Tank Battalion, landed at Guadalcanal on August 7, 1942. They encountered no opposition and merely accompanied the infantry as they carefully picked their way across the Tenaru River to set up a defensive perimeter around the Lunga Point airfield. The tanks generally remained scattered around the airfield for security and were available for counterattacks as part of the division reserve while the operation developed. Across the sound at Tulagi, however, terrain prevented much use of C Company, 2d Tank Battalion in the five separate landings made there. Little Tanambogo Island proved such a hornet's nest of resistance, though, that the landing failed and a second attempt had to be made on the second day of the assault. Two M3 tanks, led by Second Lieutenant Robert J. Sweeney, landed from 45ft tank lighters in advance of I Company, 3d Battalion, 2d Marines. As each tank worked along one side of the hilltop islet, Lieutenant Sweeney was killed by small arms fire and the tank disabled, but it continued to cover the advancing infantry. The other tank continued ahead of the infantry against a pillbox and was swarmed over by Japanese defenders, who disabled the tank's track with an iron bar and set it on fire with fuel-soaked rags. The tank crew fought hand to hand until their infantry finally closed the distance and secured the area. Two of the crew died and two others suffered severe wounds. But 42 dead Japanese ringed the tank.

Tank–infantry cooperation seemed nonexistent at this point, but the existing doctrine for tank employment as evolved in the 1930s had only called for tanks to clear the beach of enemy emplacements and little thought had been given to the precise techniques that the troops would employ. Moreover, the troops had received little training. Colonel Clifton Cates, commanding the 1st Marines, said his troops "had less than three months of battalion training ... Not once have we had a regimental problem, much less training with planes, tanks, and other units."

Benjamin W. Pugsley was the gunner of tank C14, which fought at Tanambogo Island. He may well be the only member still living of the five men who survived that action on August 8:

> We hit the beach under heavy small arms fire and proceeded toward a group of buildings a short distance from the landing point. I was firing by tracers [aiming] through a periscope and had a good view of action in front of us ... We became immobilized and could not move. At this point I noticed the turret was open and that the Japanese were trying desperately to reach inside. Sergeant Richert [the tank commander] was in a crouch position to avoid the enemy attack and yelled for the Thompson. The gun was passed to him and as he started to use the weapon a hand grenade was tossed into the tank and exploded near the top of the turret rather than falling to the bottom of the tank. Sgt. Richert took the full blast and was killed instantly.

The remaining three crewmen bailed out the drivers' hatches and fought the Japanese hand to hand as the marine riflemen rushed up to finish the fight. Although not all the engagements with light tanks ended up as poorly as the first one, the marine tankers struggled to fight in the cramped little tanks, many of which (the M2A4 and M3) had no power traverse for the turrets. While the driver and assistant driver, sitting forward in the hull, looked through vision slits and possible targets for their fixed-wing machine guns and the ball-mounted bow machine gun, the two men in the turret – gunner and commander/loader – hopped over the drive shaft and other appendages on the turret floor, cranking the turret right and left, and making the final lay of the 37mm gun and coaxial machine gun using a shoulder yoke with limited traverse and elevation and either a telescope or periscopic gun sight. Range estimation was by guess, but there were few opportunities for distant firing in the Pacific war.

Only when C Company, 1st Tank Battalion, arrived at Guadalcanal with its regiment detached from Samoa did the M3A1 light tank, with power traverse (15-second revolution) and an elevation stabilizer, come into action and reduce the typical workload of the crew. Although only two tank companies served in the crucial first three months of the Guadalcanal campaign, a total of five eventually served, and three platoons of defense battalion tanks assisted army troops in clearing the New Georgia chain next up the Solomons "Slot."

As difficult as the M3 series light tanks were to operate and fight, the Corps tried to keep its Marmon-Herrington tanks in use, forming two separate tank companies in the summer of 1942, when the vehicles had

A: US Marine Corps tanker, spring 1943

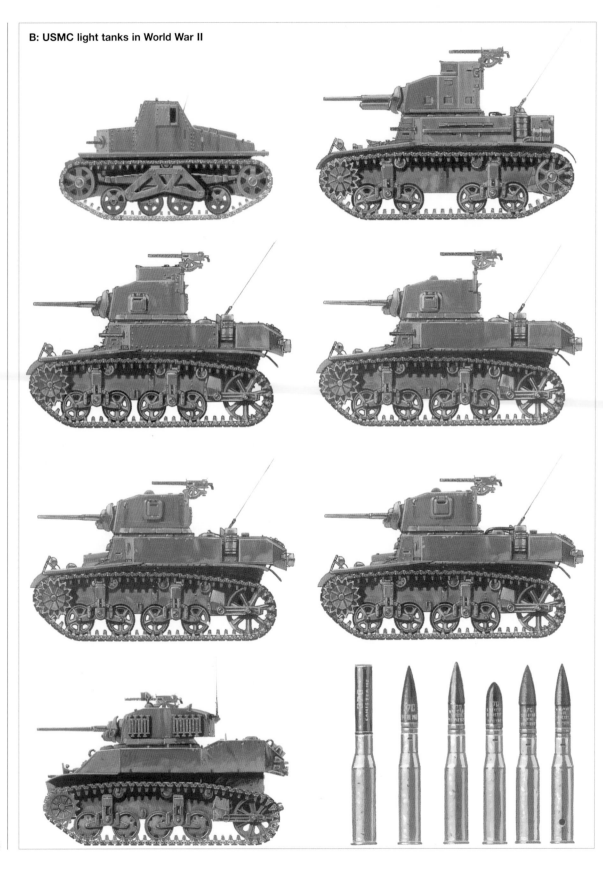

C: Training scene

C

D: Leo Case's platoon at the Battle of Tenaru

F: Battle scene, Tinian, July 25, 1944

F

G: After the battle; standing down

been rejected by the tank battalion commanders as unfit for combat. These companies went to Samoa, replacing M3-equipped tank companies needed by their parent battalions. Thankfully, these machines remained out of combat, as the Japanese threat to Samoa and the nearby Wallis Island group never materialized. Eventually, the separate companies would join new tank battalions, after receiving real tanks for combat use.

By the time the last of the battalions equipped only with light tanks went into action at Bougainville, the Marine Corps had already taken action to procure the medium tanks of the M4 series, as reinforcement for amphibious landings. The navy still lacked landing craft capable of carrying these 33 tonners, nor did anyone wish to attempt to load them into landing craft from transports anchored in a seaway using cargo booms, block, and tackle. So the Marine Corps proposed placing medium tanks into two corps medium-tank battalions, corresponding to the I (later V) and III amphibious corps being prepared for the Pacific war. These battalions would land from the new tank landing ships (LST) entering service. These large beaching vessels would come into the beach after the assault troops had passed through, unloading the mediums through their bow ramps. In the end, only one such corps tank battalion formed, in January 1943, and its four companies were designated to support different marine divisions in upcoming battles.

Bougainville was so swampy and shipping in such short supply that the new M4A2 medium tanks of B Company, 1st Corps Tank Battalion, remained back at Guadalcanal, now a rear training base, while A and B Companies landed and faced the almost impenetrable jungles and crude trails that quickly turned into muddy morasses in the tropical showers. The crews struggled mightily to gain access to the infantry front lines and provide support in what became mostly defensive actions against an elusive opponent. But Marine Corps tankers were about to leave the jungle fight.

Fred and his pals from Iceland arrived back in California just in time to ship out for New Caledonia and rejoin their battalion before the assault on Tarawa. Fred went to the 2d platoon, C Company, now wearing the corporal stripes that he might have received two years earlier had he stayed on sea duty. There was little training possible on New Caledonia, like most of the rear areas in the Pacific war. Mostly, there was maintenance, conditioning hikes, and more maintenance. The guns had not been fired in over six months. Fred had left his now ancient M2A4 in Iceland and thought the M3A1 was a Cadillac by comparison.

Learning to fight

From on board his ship 10 miles offshore, Fred could see Betio, the main island of Tarawa atoll, as a low line of land totally shrouded in gray smoke, as bombs and navy shells pummeled the island and fighter planes swooped low on their strafing runs. After watching the navy lower his tank into the LCM-3 landing craft, he and the crew of C22 scrambled down the cargo netting and dropped into the well. Taking up positions in their tank (Fred was now a gunner), they bobbed in the seaway as they made what became the longest distance assault transit of the Pacific war. With five other landing craft (they had one of the company headquarters tanks with them), the little squadron searched for a way

Why the diesel M4A2?

To this day, many veteran tankers of the World War II USMC believe that they received the diesel-engine M4A2 for compatibility with the fuel supply for landing craft marine diesels. But the fact is that the more numerous amphibious tractors had gasoline engines. The reality was simpler. Attending the November 28, 1942 International Tank Committee meeting at the War Department, Marine Corps delegates learned that production of the M4A1 and A3 would go on a priority to the British and the US armies, with the British forced to take some A4s as well. Other A4s would be used as training vehicles in the United States. An earlier protocol had slated the twin-diesel M4A2 for the Russians, who would take no other version in their Lend-Lease allocation. Amid all this competition for tanks, the Marine Corps representatives found that they could get the M4A2 earlier than any other model. They therefore recommended the procurement of 112 M4A2 tanks, plus 56 replacement tanks, in order to meet the initial requirement for the two corps medium tank battalions scheduled for standing up in January and March. Ordnance Section chief Lieutenant-Colonel John Blanchard noted to his quartermasters a few days before the 1 Corps Medium Tank Battalion activated:
"22 M4A4 at TC-SD [training command, San Diego]. 168 M4A2 ordered to SD for 1st/2d Tk. Bns. (med) [one of few references to the number of medium tank battalions planned], 40 actually arrived. 168 M4A2 allocation proposed for March. Deliver by priority rating. Do not believe M4A1 or M4A3 will be available by March or April. Since initial issue to 1st and 2d battalions will not all require replacement at same time, seems impractical to switch to new model, even if available. Model was changed from M4A4 to M4A2. British have committed to accepting ALL M4A4 tanks produced. They consider them combat-worthy."

Tankers of the 2d Separate Tank Company rest after their initial combat action at Eniwetok. Having thankfully left their Marmon-Herrington tankettes on Samoa, they drew M4A2 medium tanks and used them against the Japanese on three islands of the atoll. Typical of the many variations in markings, this tank shows the beginning of a camouflage scheme, a name on the turret side, and the USMC registration number and emblem on the hull side, probably in dull yellow. (US Coast Guard (USCG) photo)

into Red Beach as part of the sixth wave of landing craft. Machine-gun fire streaked across the water and the coxswains stayed low in their little shelter of a cockpit. Then came the splash of mortar rounds nearby; first one and then two of the other landing craft closer to the reef took direct hits. They went down like stones and the crewmen just barely managed to jump off their tanks. One more landing craft sank as the surviving craft beat a retreat back to the transport. It was a close call. Not until late the next day did Fred's tank and the platoon leader's manage to get ashore.

What he saw when he did get there was as close to hell as he ever wanted to come. Shattered landing craft and amtracs littered the beach. Four of the M4 mediums squatted in the deep water, washed out. Groups of men huddled under the coconut-log sea wall, tending casualties or operating radios. Fred only learned later that many of the tanks were knocked out the first day as they slowly picked their way ashore or ran parallel to the beach to avoid running over the bodies of marines cut down in the first waves of the day. Further inland, shells were falling everywhere and groups of marines could be seen behind dunes or in shell holes, firing into the smoke, at what, he did not know yet. After linking up with two more tanks from B Company, the platoon set out to support the 1st Battalion, 8th Marines. A mortar hit jammed one of the B Company turrets and only three light tanks lurched forward. The infantry directed Fred's tank commander to a pillbox. The tank drove right up to it, and Fred pumped HE (high explosive) shells directly into the embrasure. But only after firing ten shells inside did Fred succeed in flushing out the enemy, who were cut down with 37mm canister fire from one of the other tanks. Elsewhere, Fred was able to do good work with his coaxial machine gun, hosing down trucks, oil drums, and buildings with armor-piercing bullets, in case any Japanese troops were hiding inside.

It was hard to find the enemy, because they held fire whenever the tanks drew near. Only the infantry could see them and they had no way to communicate with Fred's platoon, since their radios operated on different frequencies. Sometimes a courageous infantry officer or NCO would jump on the turret and point out a target to the commander; Fred heard one man cry out as he was hit and knocked off the turret. Two days later, it was over. Fred's tank, six other lights and two surviving mediums reached the farthest tip of the island. But everybody saw that it was the medium tanks, with their 75mm guns, that were doing most of the damage against the bunkers and pillboxes. It was clear that the 37mm and the light tanks were not up to the mission at hand.

The early landings in the Solomons had been unopposed and the fighting mostly defensive. But assaulting central Pacific islands introduced marines to small, highly fortified and well-defended zones that had to be cleared by close assault from the first yard to the last. The officers surveying Tarawa discovered hundreds of mines not yet laid on the lagoon approaches, which had received the last priority for the garrison's work effort. Unbelievable as it seemed, things could have been worse. The Japanese surely would make improvements to their defense schemes, based upon their own lessons drawn from the battle. The amphibious art simply had to improve or the war would seemingly last forever.

For the tankers, the medium tank became the first cure to the problem, augmented later by a flame-thrower tank for close-in work. Of the 14 M4A2 tanks landing at Tarawa, only two survived the action, but they had made the difference. Once C Company, 1st Corps Medium Tank Battalion, had recovered, it was added to the 2d Tank Battalion as its new A Company. A similar move for the 1st Tank Battalion, then training in Australia, brought 22 army-issue M4A1 tanks for issue, with spares, to its own A Company. Thus Bougainville became the last USMC amphibious assault by light tanks alone, and the Corps moved to a mixed battalion of one company with medium and two with light tanks. The companies, like the divisional battalions, were never designated "light" or "medium" as was the case in the US Army. Only the table of organization and equipment issued to them made the difference. Ironically, the Corps had just placed a massive order with the army for the latest light tanks – 735 of the new M5A1 light tanks – but few would come into service. In January 1944, just before departing the US for the invasion of Roi-Namur (Kwajalein Islands), the 4th Tank Battalion converted one company to medium tanks. The Corps was officially committed to mixed medium and light tanks in the divisional battalions, and the 1st Corps Tank Battalion disbanded in February.

The Battle for Roi-Namur saw the medium tanks handling all but the largest concrete and log fortifications, and the new M5A1 light tanks, much improved over the old M3s, still had only the 37mm gun and could not cross the rough terrain that the medium handled so well. When the 2d Separate Tank Company, at last freed from Samoa defense

After the fighting ceased on Betio (Tarawa), the salvageable tanks were repaired and refitted for the next operation. Two M4A2 mediums and four M3A1 light tanks appear in good shape two months later, the near M4A2 showing the elephant logo of the 1st Corps Medium Tank Battalion, later adopted by 3d Tank Battalion. (USN photo)

duty, annihilated several Japanese light Type 95 tanks on Eniwetok Atoll, the die was cast. All tank units converted to medium for the summer campaign in the Marianas.

In stark contrast to Fred's experiences at Tarawa, where a marine regiment was almost exterminated on the beach, the Battle for Saipan was a tanker's dream. A large island, Saipan afforded room to maneuver and mostly good trafficability for tanks as well. Still in C Company, Fred was a sergeant commanding C22, now a powerful M2A4 medium tank, powered by twin diesels and manned by a crew of five (commander, gunner, loader, driver, assistant driver). The tank crew coordination now came into its own with the M4 series tank, which marines never called a "Sherman," just "medium" or "M4" until the British-inspired nickname caught on after the war. A true weapons system, the medium tank required quick, sequential actions by all the crew members while operating or fighting it.

The driver and assistant driver sat at the left and right side of the bow, or forward hull of the tank. The transmission lay between them and, as there had been no dual controls provided in any US tank since the Marmon-Herrington (until the army M26 of 1945), the term "assistant driver" really had no meaning. The second crewman simply handled the bow machine gun, in its ball mounting, and attempted to fire using the tracers and looking

through the same type of periscope as the driver. The fixed periscope replaced the vision slit on the older tanks and the early M4s. The overhead hatch at each forward position also had its own periscope, rotating in a full circle and tilting to raise or lower the view. The driver operated a switch and instrument panel controlling the engine, and used steering levers to turn and brake the machine, a foot accelerator and clutch on the floor and a gearshift to the right to move the 35-ton tank in its five forward and one reverse gears.

In the center or fighting compartment, seated in a "basket" rotating with the rest of the turret, the remainder of the crew operated the main weapons and radios. Tucked forward on the right, next to the gun, sat the gunner, who used his choice of a periscope or telescope sight to aim the 75mm cannon and the coax machine gun. Using various handles and switches, he could elevate the gun manually and traverse the turret with either hydraulic power or the old manual hand crank. Separate triggers for the coax and main gun completed the controls. There was also a power elevation stabilizer that some crews operated but most declined to use, according to several accounts. On the other side of the gun sat the loader, who had to locate the correct ammunition type, of several carried, and load the 75mm gun as rapidly as possible, while keeping an eye on the Browning .30 caliber coax to see that it was functioning correctly and still had plenty of ammo feeding into the machine gun with cloth belts from a feedbox mounted on the turret side. He also had to assist the tank commander in operating the radio sets in the turret rear. By 1944, these were army SCR-508A and 528A sets (equal except the SCR-508A had two receivers to permit listening on separate radio nets).

As the tank commander, Fred reported to his platoon commander for everything to do with his tank. The maintenance, training, provisioning, discipline, and tactical movement of the tank were his alone to perform, with the help of his crew and the assigned maintenance and supply sections of C Company. In action, he would have to maintain radio communications with his platoon leader, while at the same time giving fire commands to the gunner and loader and movement directions to the driver over the intercom. In his "TC" position, he also had the best view of what was going on outside and therefore had to keep aware of what the enemy and friendly troops and machines were doing. Fred learned fast, thanks to the veteran platoon leader he worked for. William Franklin McMillian, Marine Gunner USMC, had enlisted in 1933 and served as a rifleman in the 4th Marines at Shanghai in 1934. He liked China so much that he stayed three enlistments, literally taking the last boat out in 1941 right before the war began. As a platoon sergeant at Camp Elliott, he was made a first sergeant in the 2d Marines. He hated paperwork, so when Captain Swencesky, another old China hand, asked him to come to his new tank company, he was more than eager to do it. After Tarawa, "Mac" received a spot promotion to second lieutenant.

On Saipan, his leadership ran over the edge. As Ed Bale, who had led the medium company at Tarawa, later related:

Mac was an unusual character. As a marine he was tough, brave, honest, and always concerned about his "boys." He wanted to be where the action was. On D-day on Saipan, Mac reported to me shortly after landing in support of the Eighth Marines. He had a towel wrapped around his throat. After giving several evasive answers, Mac admitted that he had been hit in the flabby skin under his chin. I told him to go back to the beach and check into an aid station for possible evacuation to an offshore ship. For several days my contact with that platoon was through the platoon sergeant. Quite by accident I learned that Mac was hiding from me inside a tank and a tank crewman was treating his wound. Mac told me he "did not want to leave his boys" and he wanted to be where the action was.

Fred and the C Company tankers had lost several friends in the landing, as the tanks came off the LCM-6 landing craft and advanced in fender-deep water across the reef to Green Beach. Unfortunately, navy shells and bombs had left large craters in the reef. One of the 2d platoon tanks went into a hole and only two heads bobbed to the surface. Further south, the 4th Tank Battalion had good and bad luck: all of C Company made it in, but A Company lost three and B Company only had four of 14 safely ashore. Linking up with the rifle companies of 8th Marines, Fred's company worked well against the weak Japanese counterattacks and the few positions encountered on D-day, because by mid-1944, all the marine divisions had worked out standard procedures for tank–infantry tactics. The tanks and infantry worked closely together, even when the tanks led the advance against heavy Japanese resistance. The rifle platoons knew to keep an eye out for sudden rushes by antitank squads armed with bottled gasoline (the famous Molotov Cocktail), satchel charges of explosives with short or instantaneous fuses, and magnetic antitank mines. As long as the riflemen picked off the Japanese with their rifles and automatic weapons, the tanks would stay in action and the partnership continue toward the objective. The tanks could protect themselves to a limited extent, sweeping each other with machine-gun fire, but the limited visibility left the main job to the infantry to keep them in action. Unlike in the European theater, tanks in the Pacific war of necessity fought buttoned up, for the main danger to them remained the suicidal rushes of Japanese infantry, not the weakly armed tanks or the few antitank guns of 47mm and larger size that they usually encountered.

Like tankers in Europe, the USMC crews strapped on extra sections of steel track to the front and turret sides of their M4s. Protection for the turret roof and crew hatches frequently took the form of nails welded to the tanks, points up. Sandbags placed on the engine tops protected against satchel charges and thrown mines. In C Company, 4th Tank Battalion, Captain Bob Neiman's inventive crews mounted "cages" of heavy mesh, rising 2in. over the hatches, preventing any direct contact with these vulnerable points by hand-placed explosives. On the sides, wood planking, 2 x 12in. wide, hung 4in. outward from the hull, with a 4in. thickness of concrete poured between planks and hull. The wood prevented use of magnetic mines and the concrete proved immune to the Japanese 47mm antitank guns.

Japanese tanks appeared on Saipan, in the largest attack of this kind encountered in the Pacific war. Approximately 44 tanks, mostly

RIGHT
Marine Corps tankers used many improvisations to ward off the explosive charges or mines used by Japanese infantry in close combat against their tanks. This M4A2 of C Company, 4th Tank Battalion, shows the spare track blocks mounted on turret side and hull front and the ingenious "bird cage" steel mesh placed over hatches to prevent direct contact with such weak points. (Author's collection)

RIGHT
One of the M32B2 tank recovery vehicles of 3d Tank Battalion hauls away a knocked-out Japanese Type 95 light tank, after another encounter between tanks on Guam. The elephant logo can be seen on the hull side of the USMC vehicle, as well as the vehicle name, "Almighty." (USMC photo)

mediums, some armed with 47mm cannon, rolled toward the lines of the 2d Marine Division early in the morning of June 17. Following them came about 500 men of an infantry regiment, hell-bent to drive a wedge into the American lines until reaching the beach, less than a mile away. However, air reconnaissance had spotted a few tanks during the day and engine sounds filled the early hours of the evening. The marines stood ready, although the night tactics of the enemy allowed the Japanese to come uncomfortably close. The Japanese tanks roared out of the darkness, but ran into "… a madhouse of noise, tracers, and flashing lights. As tanks were hit and set afire, they silhouetted other tanks coming out of the flickering shadows to the front or already on top of the [rifle] squads." Most of the attack fell upon the lines of the 6th Marines, and Captain Frank Stewart's B Company handled many of the Japanese tanks, taking care not to fire into friendly infantry, which probably destroyed the majority of enemy tanks with their bazookas and regimental antitank guns. Marine tankers began to recognize that their armor-piercing projectiles were passing clean through the lightly armored Japanese vehicles, sometimes leaving them in action, and so

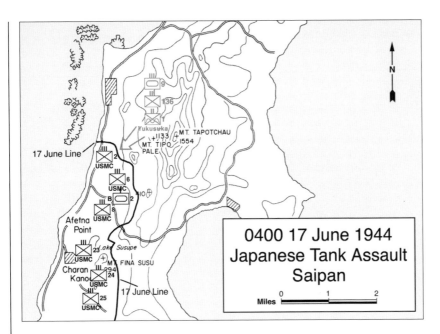

0400 17 June 1944 Japanese Tank Assault Saipan

Miles 0 1 2

they switched to high-explosive 75mm ammo to make their hits count. Three-quarters of the enemy tanks remained on the battlefield as smoldering hulks.

Fred and his C22 crew heard the engine and track noises of the Japanese tank counterattack. The firing went on for two hours, but his sector with 8th Marines remained fairly quiet, and his platoon was not called forward to the lines. The next morning, his platoon moved out, slightly ahead of the infantry. The Japanese still had lots of fight left in them and opened up from a treeline. Fred went first into the attack, finding the area swarming with Japanese, who had no antitank weapons, just machine guns and mortars. As the 6th Marines riflemen came up, Fred engaged the enemy for an hour or so, his gunner shooting the hell out of them with the 75mm, using HE ammo, and kept the coax machine gun continuously chattering, moving slowly through. His loader kept squirting oil on the ammo belts as they disappeared into the Browning M37, a trick they had learned to use whenever they pushed the gun beyond what the "book" told them were its limits. Eventually, the gun ended up white-hot, cooking off a round every minute or so without pressing the trigger, until Fred had the loader pull the rounds out of the cloth belt.

While the fight was going on, Fred noticed a single Japanese infantryman setting

up a tripod up the road. He was sure that the soldier must have an AT weapon of some sort, else why would he be setting up in the road? His gunner was shooting up some target on the left side and Fred tried to get his attention, but he couldn't make himself heard over the intercom. Kicking the gunner several times finally got the message across. Both men could now see that the Japanese soldier had set up a Nambu machine gun. Fred's gunner killed him right away with his coax, thinking what a futile gesture for that soldier. C22 and the rest of the platoon eventually worked through the woodline, killing more Japanese soldiers that day than on any other in the war. Yet only a few thousand yards to the south of them, Gunnery Sergeant McCard had fought to the death against Japanese infantry, to save his crew bailing out of a crippled M4A2 tank. You had to have luck, too, to survive this kind of fighting.

Try as they might, the tankers could contribute little to the fighting in the mountainous center of the island, because tanks could not follow their infantry. Neither could the two improvised "D" companies of "Satan" flame-thrower tanks brought with the two marine tank battalions, the last use to be made of the light tank by the Corps. This conversion mounted a Canadian Ronson flame-thrower in the M3A1 turret, with 170gal. of thickened flame fuel, projected by compressed carbon dioxide to a range of 60–80yd for up to two minutes of use. Of course, the "Satan" retained the weak armor of the base vehicle, while the flame equipment limited the turret traverse to 10 degrees left and 80 degrees right of center. These machines performed well in mopping up rear area resistance, but had little role in the main fighting.

Veteran tankers in action

The same divisions landed on nearby Tinian and found excellent tank country, once the narrow beaches and hills fronting them had been passed on July 24, 1944. The flat cane fields concealed some of the few defenders and antitank guns left after a foolish charge of the Japanese mobile reserves the first night. The seasoned tank–infantry teams secured the island in a single week. Guam, the last major objective of the Marianas campaign, revealed mixed terrain like Saipan, but not as severe. The tanks of 3d Tank Battalion and two separate tank companies

Marine infantry provide security to tanks of C Company, 4th Tank Battalion, as they advance through the cane fields southward toward Tinian town. The procedure called "support by fire" required a squad of riflemen to watch over each tank and shoot down any Japanese infantrymen trying to use pole charges, mines or satchel charges to knock out the tank. All the USMC divisions had adopted these and other tank–infantry tactics by mid-1944. (USMC photo)

working with the 1st Marine Brigade waded ashore without incident. A major night counterattack hit the marines here as at Saipan, but the 38 Japanese tanks failed to concentrate and instead fought piecemeal throughout the 20-day battle, with about a dozen of them falling to USMC tank cannon.

Having shifted from the thick jungle islands of the southwest Pacific, to coral atolls of the central Pacific, and then mastering the plains, mountains, and jungle islands of the larger western Pacific islands, Marine Corps tankers now faced a shifting tactical doctrine of their determined foe. Having lost heavily with its tactics of massed "banzai" charges into the prepared American defenses, the Japanese Army now adopted a defense in depth, relying upon well-prepared fortifications and tenacious infantry defense to cause attrition and weaken the attackers. The 1st Marine Division encountered the new doctrine at Peleliu, where they landed on September 15. At first, the Japanese seemed to fight in the old way. Blockhouses and pillboxes on the beach fired against the amtrac-mounted infantry and accompanying tanks (only 30 landed, owing to shipping shortages) as they crossed the wide reef ringing the island. The Japanese defenders knew from previous reports that they had to stop the Marine Corps armored vehicles. Only three tanks were disabled, but 26 amtracs burned as the tank–infantry teams spread out to take on the numerous surviving fortified positions. In the late afternoon, the Japanese commander launched his single planned counterattack, a battalion of infantry and his 15 light tanks, kept concealed in the high ground in the island's center. This deliberate attack, not a banzai charge, came far too late to save his beach defenses. The marine battalions were on line to receive the attack. All weapons came to bear on this new threat and it was annihilated – all but perhaps two of the Japanese Type 95 light tanks were destroyed and the accompanying infantrymen chewed up. Once again, the marine tanks had to share the count with the gun crews and riflemen.

The rest of the battle was another thing, however. The tenaciously defended caves and fortified positions of the rugged interior of the island resisted all but the most desperate assaults. Bulldozers and tank dozers cut paths for the US tanks to approach the Japanese positions, but the Japanese exerted a fierce attrition with their artillery and mortars on the marine riflemen. Tankers and

The Japanese tank attack at Peleliu surprised the attacking Marine Corps battalions, and the commander of the 1st Tank Battalion surmised that the Japanese commander must have thought the USMC tanks had not been landed. Two platoons of M4A2 tanks, one on the beach and another advancing across the airfield, proved more than equal to the task. (Map by W. Stephen Hill from US Army original)

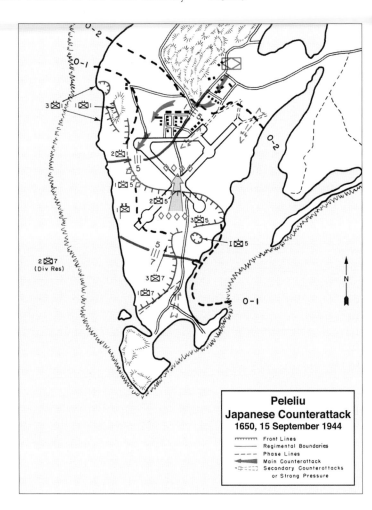

Peleliu
Japanese Counterattack
1650, 15 September 1944

Front Lines
Regimental Boundaries
Phase Lines
Main Counterattack
Secondary Counterattacks or Strong Pressure

riflemen alike collapsed under the humid tropical heat, and in the end army troops had to be brought in to complete the mopping-up of the island. The new look in Japanese defenses bode ill for the rest of the Pacific war: there remained many islands to overrun in the Japanese Empire.

None of these events came to Fred's attention, as he and his crew rested after the Tinian battle and wondered what would come next. The island campaign in the Pacific war had a strange rhythm to it, with amphibious assaults often short and extremely violent, followed by a re-embarkation into shipping to the Hawaiian Islands or a captured island for rest and recovery. Some outfits lucked out, as in the case of the 4th Marine Division. After leaving the US to attack Roi-Namur, it returned after every battle to Maui, where it was practically adopted by the civilian population. With a tank park on the beach, away from the main divisional bivouac area, the 4th Tank Battalion tankers could work and relax well removed from most critical eyes. At the other extreme, the 1st Marine Division drew Pavuvu, a desolate and isolated island in the Russell Islands that turned to mud under the frequent torrents of tropical rain. Australia, their refit locale after Guadalcanal, was only a dream after the division's second campaign on New Britain, when Pavuvu became their "home." Amid tens of thousands of rotting, stinking coconuts and maybe a lesser number of sand crabs, the marines struggled to keep their tent cities dry and improve the roads and trails.

Fred and his pals languished on Saipan, fortunate to be in the mainstream of supply as the army and navy built the Marianas into forward bases and depots supporting the rest of the campaign. The 3d Marine Division drew Guam as a forward base and, while not Maui, it also was not Pavuvu or Guadalcanal, where the new 6th Marine Division had gathered. Fred had seen almost all of the possibilities with the 2d Tank Battalion since they had reformed after Tarawa on the island of Hawaii,

During the fight for Peleliu, tanks and infantry crossed to nearby Ngesebus Island on September 28, 1944, taking advantage of low tide to cross shore to shore. Sixteen of the 19 operable M4A2 tanks carried out this operation, including the last of the invaluable dozer tanks. (USMC photo)

One of the camps on Guadalcanal, more peaceful now as a rear area base, but easily saturated by the monsoon rains. This is a "main street" in the rainy season. (USMC photo)

at the Parker Ranch Marine Corps camp, christened Camp Tarawa. But the new 5th Marine Division now occupied it and, unlike the 4th, they could not return. Fred sure regretted missing New Zealand, but he had still served on Iceland when the division had first sailed from the west coast.

Fred now found himself promoted to platoon sergeant and, since C Company already had its quota, he said goodbye to Gunner McMillian and reported to A Company, commanded by Captain Ed Bale, the gritty, tough Texan who had taken the first M4s into combat at Tarawa. Everybody now had their hands full, because the new tanks had arrived as part of their refit – and they were different! Once again, the Corps had changed models, this time to the M4A3, with its 450hp Ford GAA gasoline engine. Nobody liked losing their trusty twin-diesel M4A2s. What had happened?

Only the Marine Corps and the Russian Army used the diesel-powered Sherman tank (a few had gone to the British), and the US Army had standardized the M4A3, with its gasoline-fueled Ford engine, for its own mass production. Furthermore, the army provided only the latest design improvements and field modifications for this model. The Marine Corps required medium tank inventory now exceeded 500 vehicles, counting training and replacement stocks. Upcoming changes in the production line threatened the Marine Corps tank fleet as well as the ammunition supply so laboriously built up in the Pacific theater. So now the Corps acquired the latest M4A3 models to equip the new 5th and 6th Tank Battalions and refurbish the remaining tank battalions with the newest but last of the M4 series production line to have the 75mm gun.

One thing Fred liked immediately about the new tank was the vision ring of several periscope blocks installed in a cupola for the tank commander's hatch. With it, he could stay buttoned up and still have a 360-degree view of the battle, except for the typical "dead space" close to the tank, where one had to worry about enemy infantry assaults. The crews quickly came to like the new gasoline engine, which was strong and reliable, even though they feared the fire hazard of gasoline that diesel engines did not have. The new tank also came with a factory-installed infantry telephone on the right rear fender, which eliminated the jury-rig field phone the tankers had been using to better communicate with the infantry teams they worked with.

Pacific island battles had an unreal rhythm: days or weeks of incomprehensible violence and danger, followed by months of recuperation in island bases thousands of miles away, where washing and bathing were part of the recuperation routine. (USMC photo)

On Tinian, Fred operated his M4A2, C22 "Comet," for the last time, here advancing through the cane with the infantry in close support, physically guarding the tank. After Tinian, the 2d Tank Battalion received M4A3 tanks. (USMC photo)

Marine riflemen advance jubilantly to the east and north after landing on Okinawa riding on an M4A3 tank of the 6th Tank Battalion. The lower exhaust section of the fording stacks remains on the tank. Note the excellent vision ring now part of the tank commander's hatch. (USMC photo)

The telephone allowed the infantry to spot and give the tankers targets, and otherwise tell them what was going on in the heat of action, without exposing themselves by climbing on the tank and banging on the hatches for attention. A Company began training with the 8th Marines for the next operation, but this time, almost a year would elapse before they saw action.

While the III Amphibious Corps, with the 1st, 2d, and 6th Marine Divisions, prepared for the invasion of Okinawa under the 10th Army, the V Amphibious Corps, with the other three divisions, landed on Iwo Jima for the Corps' largest and most bloody island battle ever. Even more than at Peleliu, the Japanese commanders resisted the old temptation to counterattack, and Iwo required the assault troops to ferret them out from their concealed and cleverly sited battle positions.

At first, the objective offered little good news for the tankers. Marine intelligence planners knew that the beach area consisted of volcanic ash, extending up past the edge of Airfield #1, the initial objective for the assault. Photos also revealed hundreds of bomb craters left by the shuttle bombing done by the air strikes, as well as some earlier ship bombardments. Unable to gauge the size of these craters, though, tankers wondered if they would be obstacles or not. There were certainly far too many of them to cross, if they did indeed turn out to be obstacles. Then, at the last minute, came some submarine periscope photos, showing some of the elevation of

These tankers of C Company, 4th Tank Battalion, on Iwo Jima have a hard day's work ahead, digging out their bogged dozer tank. Note the improvised protection: timber sides, sandbags over the engine armor, and birdcage hatch covers. The cylindrical light tank auxiliary fuel cell was filled with water for distribution to the infantry they supported. (Author collection)

the terrain that could not be seen in the overhead aerial photography. Two terraces, each about 20yd or more wide, fronted the beach, but nobody knew their height or could estimate whether they would be obstacles. So now a lot of unknowns faced the marines embarked for the invasion, but the first priority was getting tanks ashore and into action.

One new solution to the Japanese defenses came in the latest flame tank, developed on the M4 chassis. One company each in 4th and 5th Tank Battalions received four

Another view of a tank of C Company, 4th Tank Battalion, on Iwo, showing how the wood planks supported a 4in. layer of reinforced concrete, making the tank proof against the Japanese 47mm antitank gun on the side. Everybody wore helmets, even in the rear area, because the Japanese artillery and mortars covered the entire island. (USMC photo)

of these. A combined army, navy, and marine team, based in Hawaii, had removed the 75mm gun and installed a flame weapon, using a worn 75mm barrel but connected by various valves and tubes to a large fuel tank and compressed air cylinders. The compressed air threw out a stream of napalm, about ¾ in. in diameter. The gunner would walk it onto the target. On the target, pressing another switch ignited the napalm and a stream of fire shot out. This tank was the answer to dealing with Japanese fortifications, which had become even tougher as marines progressed across the Pacific (see plate G).

Landing from his LSM (landing ship, medium) in the middle of the division zone, Major Bob Neiman guided his C Company, 4th Tank Battalion across the terraced volcanic ash.

All we had to do was line up and zig-zag over two collapsed spots and all of a sudden, the entire company was on the flat, with [guide] Cpl. Jewell still leading, on foot. We skirted the bomb craters, continuing across the waist of the island. The smoke and noise prevented me from seeing much more than Jewell, but then we came upon some infantry, all hugging the deck, and this told me that the enemy lay ahead. I sent Jewell back. Ahead, looking though my periscopes, I could make out 7–8 pillboxes, on a line roughly blocking our direction of advance. Now we could go to work! The platoons swung by, and they began to work over the pillboxes with 75mm cannon and machine guns. The new flame tanks closed the distance and I was immediately impressed with their effect. When the flame hit the pillbox, the Japanese would usually break and run, and we cut them down with our machine guns.

We destroyed all the pillboxes and proceeded uphill with the infantry following to the airfield. An embankment separated the approach slope from the level plain of the airfield, and after a quick look up on the flat, I reformed the company behind this embankment, in order to rearm and count noses with some cover from the direct fire which whizzed around the island at any time. The infantry dug in on the edge of the airfield, so we had a relatively secure position at that point. The night proved a difficult one, as the heavy artillery fire really gave us no rest. The Japanese fired all calibers of weapons and really didn't need to target anything specifically. The two divisions crowded into the narrowest part of the island presented a perfect area target. We particularly worried about the large spigot mortars and the 'screaming mimie' rocket projectiles. But in the end, these proved far less deadly than the constant rain of mortar bombs and light artillery shells, which the Japanese seemed to have in unlimited supply. Then the ammo dump went up. Resting in the hole we had dug under my tank, I thought it was some of my tanks next to me blowing up and imagined all kinds of catastrophes happening. Surely we had arrived in Hell.

The hell lasted another six weeks. The tanks accompanied the infantry through almost all terrain, again carving trails with dozer tanks to reach the interior caves. At one point, all the usable tanks of the three battalions, 3d, 4th, and 5th, were combined after the last division had landed, and they massed in a single tank attack across the second of the three airfields against the Motoyama Plateau and the main line of Japanese resistance. Almost 100 tanks went into action that day, a record number for the Pacific war, but the mines, antitank guns, and broken terrain robbed the attack of its mass. Instead, it took three more days for the tanks and rifle squads to pick their way across the open ground. Bob Neiman lost track of the days, as the battle dragged on:

> The enemy had to be literally dug out of his rocky lair by teams of infantry companies and small numbers of tanks. Often we had to use tank dozers or armored bulldozers to cut a path for the gun and flame tanks to follow.
>
> We had more than a few misunderstandings from the infantry as we poured fire into the enemy positions only to pull back when we ran out of ammo. The expressions of the infantry were pitiful and they yelled to us to stay. When we explained that we were only going back for more ammunition and would be right back (really an hour or more would be lost), they calmed down and understood.

Reducing these last positions took until late March, and small actions continued even after the V Corps had left the island. The 9th Marines' after-action report concluded the obvious: "The most effective supporting weapon in this action was the tank." But only a few days later came the "last battle" of the Great Pacific War, Okinawa, with the final development of Marine Corps tank doctrine, equipment and tactics. Landing on April 1, the marines at first ran wild to the north of the landing site. The 6th Marine Division, in particular, pushed reconnaissance troops riding on tanks up the narrow roads. The 1st Marine Division cleared the central part of the island and was first called into the 10th Army lines in the south, where the Japanese commander had prepared the now doctrinal last-stand redoubt.

On the beach at Iwo, men of 5th Tank Battalion dig out the suspension in the volcanic ash to repair mine damage. This battalion also used planking on the sides and employed a camouflage pattern using tan bands. (USMC photo)

The III Amphibious Corps entered the decisive southern battles on May 6, with the 1st Marine Division assaulting the "Shuri Heights" and the 6th taking on "Sugar Loaf." Thus began a virtual repeat of the attrition battle for Iwo, but with only two marine divisions in line with five of the army. In the attrition war for successive ridgelines fought by the soldiers and marines until June 23, the tanks and flame-thrower tanks pressed their weight wherever feasible or wherever roads could be hacked using bulldozers and tank dozers. Artillery and air support could seldom find or neutralize the Japanese positions for any amount of time. When the tanks could approach the enemy lines, they operated ahead of the infantry, but close enough to receive protective fire from squads assigned to cover each vehicle. This measure stymied the Japanese close assault squads from using their lethal mines and satchel charges. Other tanks "overwatched" from the heights, looking for the telltale smoke of an antitank gun firing on the advancing vehicles.

In the 1st Tank Battalion, the standard tank–infantry attacks against the Japanese positions became known as "processing." Lieutenant-Colonel Arthur J. Stuart explained that this most successful employment tactic

> … against enemy fortress defensive areas, has consisted of the point <u>destruction</u> of emplacements by tanks, covered by [infantry] fire teams prior to a general advance. Tanks range out to positions up to 800 yards beyond our front lines, destroying positions on forward <u>and reverse</u> slopes within that distance, chiefly by point 75mm gun fire (appropriate shell and fuse settings) at cave entrances, apertures, OP's and likely locations of same. In addition, tanks <u>destroy</u> in a similar fashion enemy direct fire positions on forward slopes for an additional 1500 yards to the front beyond the farthest point of tank advance. Repeated relays of tanks are necessary. This "processing" then permits the infantry to advance lines under cover of neutralization fires of all

types some 500 yards forward with relatively light losses and hold the ground. The procedure is then repeated in a zone extended further to the front. Japanese close assault tank hunters in spider holes, etc., employing both thrown satchel charges and strapped-on suicide demolition charges (both covered by enemy smoke) have been repeatedly encountered and necessitated positive infantry coverage … most effectively provided by our superb infantry – as evidenced by the fact that not a single tank while in action (not abandoned) has been stopped or destroyed by tank hunters during the Palau and Okinawa operations, in spite of innumerable and varied attempts.

After Okinawa had fallen, the two Marine Amphibious Corps prepared for the two invasions of the main islands of Japan. Yet another set of new tanks began to arrive at the forward bases, and again the tankers had a shock. They were new production M4A3 tanks, but now armed with a 105mm howitzer in place of the trusty 75mm tank cannon. In 1945, the army intended to replace the M4 as the standard production tank with the new T26 medium tank, with its 90mm gun. M4A3 production would continue, but only with the new 105mm howitzer turret, intended as a close support tank for infantry. Marine Corps requirements for replacement M4 series tanks in 1945 forced it to accept the 105mm gun tanks. These continued in postwar service, along with a new model flame tank, in which the main gun (75mm or 105mm) was retained and the flame gun was placed alongside it.

THE AFTERMATH

Fred and his crew never had to test the 105mm M4 tank in action, and they were glad of that. Instead, they landed at Sasebo on occupation

Two crews of B Company, 1st Tank Battalion, are using a lubrication unit during a lull in the Battle of Okinawa. This battalion worked against the supply "system" and was able to keep their late-model twin-diesel M4A2 tanks through the end of the war. (USMC photo)

duty. Fred had lots of service "points" earned since his early enlistment, and was one of the first to be sent home. In the process of thinning out, the 2d and 5th Marine Divisions and their tankers merged into the former, and these troops remained only a year before shipping out for the US and reorganization at Camp Lejeune, North Carolina, its home base ever since. The tankers of the 1st and 6th Tank Battalions remained longer, for their divisions went to north China to take the Japanese surrender there, separate them from the Chinese, and repatriate them. Apart from a few actions against Chinese "bandits," it was routine duty and ended with the evacuation of Americans from Tsingtao in 1947.

Like so many other survivors of the Pacific war, Fred never looked back. He took his discharge and went to work as a mechanic, ending up owning his own garage in Portland. He married in 1947, and saw his three children and seven grandchildren grow up before he passed away in 1998. Like so many of his generation, Fred did what he had to do, questioning little, and after the war figured that life was for the living and stayed busy with his work. He thought it curious that his grandchildren wanted to know what he had done in the war, because he thought everybody had served the same way and that there was nothing exceptional about his experience. Before he died, he began to understand the growing public interest in who the veterans were and how they had fought the war. It never ceased to amaze him.

The same could not be said for many of Fred's comrades. Although tank casualties proved fewer than in the infantry, they were equally egregious. Psychiatric casualties had mounted in the furious island battles of the central and western Pacific, especially Peleliu, Iwo and Okinawa. The incidence of amputations remained high, for the tankers suffered from the appalling effects of shell and armor

The crew of "Killer," an M4A2 of C Company, 4th Tank Battalion, on Namur, pose with their tank loaded with a trophy, a Japanese Type 94 tankette. They wear P1941 HBT utilities, standard armor force helmets, Resistol goggles, and boondocker boots. Pistols in shoulder holsters and the Thompson M1A1 with drum magazine are their individual weapons. The crewman second from left has cut his HBT trousers into shorts. (USMC photo)

fragments flung around the interiors of hulls and turrets that had been penetrated by Japanese 47mm and 75mm cannon. The catastrophic loss of entire tanks with their crews at Iwo and Okinawa would remain vividly etched in the memories of many tankers. Some would even remember the screams of a crew burning up in a tank of 6th Tank Battalion, overturned by a mine on Okinawa. Medical attention had improved by the war's end, especially with the availability of sulfa drugs. But the problems of evacuating casualties from a tank disabled or wrecked under direct enemy fire were never solved. Too many friends were lost.

Several members of Fred's old platoon returned to the Corps for the Korean War, and they told him of finding other familiar faces. G. M. English, now a captain, took the first tank company to deploy to Korea into the Pusan perimeter, with the provisional brigade sent there. Mr McMillian was the maintenance officer of the 1st Tank Battalion, and became a platoon leader for a while in "GM's" company. Ed Bale was the final battalion commander, who shipped it out of Korea and back to California. Then there was Alexander Swencesky, who took command of the 7th Tank Battalion, a wartime mobilization outfit that replaced the 1st Battalion when it went overseas. Shortly before Fred died, the Marine Corps named its annual tank gunnery competition and trophy after Bob McCard.

MUSEUMS AND COLLECTIONS

The major government collections containing tanks used by the Marine Corps are:

The Patton Museum, Fort Knox (http://www.armorfortheages.com/);

The Ordnance Museum, Aberdeen Proving Ground
  (http://www.ordmusfound.org/); and

The Marine Corps Air and Ground Museum (closed to convert to the
  National Marine Corps Museum at Quantico, Virginia
  (http://www.usmcmuseum.org/Store/MCHF/index.asp).

Private collections usually contain only one or two relevant examples, usually M3A1, M5A1, and M4A3 vehicles. No M2A4 light tanks appear to have survived the war. Jacques Littlefield's extensive private collection (http://www.milvehtechfound.com/index.html) may include one of the nine M1917A1 light tanks from the prewar experimental platoon, and the American Society of Military History Museum at South El Monte, California (http://members.aol.com/tankland/museum.htm), has the chassis of a USMC CTL-3. Other collections include Allan Cors' Virginia Museum of Military Vehicles (http://www.vmmv.org/), which opens only for scheduled displays, and the American Armored Force Museum (http://www.aaftankmuseum.com/Tank_Museum.htm). The M4A2 and M4A4 variants of the medium tank remain relatively rare, but the rest of the vehicles used in USMC service can be found in most major collections.

Few museums have acquired examples of tanker apparel and personal gear, and reenactment groups remain relatively rare, apart from certain open houses performed by the museums and private collections.

BIBLIOGRAPHY

Estes, Kenneth W., *Marines Under Armor: The Marine Corps and the Armored Fighting Vehicle, 1916–2000,* Naval Institute Press, Annapolis, 2000

Estes, Kenneth W., and Neiman, Robert M., *Tanks on the Beach: a Marine Corps Tanker in the Great Pacific War, 1941–1946,* Texas A&M University Press, College Station, 2003

Gilbert, Oscar E., *Marine Tank Battles in the Pacific,* DaCapo Press, Conshohocken, 2001

Green, Michael, *M4 Sherman,* Motorbooks International, Osceola WI, 1993

Halberstadt, Hans, *Inside the Great Tanks,* Crowood Press, London, 1997

Metzger, Louis, "Duty Beyond the Seas," in *Marine Corps Gazette,* January, 1982, pp. 28–37

Moran, Jim, *U.S. Marine Corps Uniforms and Equipment in World War II,* Motorbooks International, Osceola WI, 1993

Tulkoff, Alec S., *Grunt Gear: USMC Combat Infantry Equipment of World War II,* Bender Publishing, San Jose, 2003

Yaffe, Bertram A., *Fragments of War,* Naval Institute Press, Annapolis, 1999

Zaloga, Steve, *Armor of the Pacific War,* Osprey, Oxford, 1983

Zaloga, Steve, *M3 & M5 Stuart Light Tank 1940–1945,* Osprey, Oxford, 2000

COLOR PLATE COMMENTARY

A: US MARINE CORPS TANKER, SPRING 1943

This tank crewman shows the typical clothing and equipment worn while on the tank in the Pacific war. The basis is the P1941 herringbone twill (HBT) utility jacket and trousers with leather boondocker boots. Although regulations specified the canvas leggings used by US Marines until after the Korean War, these remained impractical at best, and even dangerous in the confines of a tank fighting compartment crammed with moving parts. Note the standard USMC and emblem stenciled on the jacket breast pocket. The tropical heat caused many tankers to wear no underwear and also to use the separate hand microphone instead of the T30D throat microphone, which tended to chafe the neck. Heat and confined spaces also limited the equipment worn by USMC tankers to that essential for self-protection when dismounted. Thus, he wears the standard pistol belt, M1916 leather holster with M1911A1 pistol, the 1942 first-aid kit, and .45 caliber magazine pouch on the belt, but no canteen or other accoutrements more easily stowed in the vehicle. Slung over his shoulder is the M1A1 Thompson submachine gun, nominally issued as one per tank, but these weapons inevitably multiplied in combat, along with shotguns, trophy weapons, and the like. He wears the Rawlings armored force helmet. The other illustrations show the M1911 pistol (.45 caliber, personal weapon of all tankers), the M1A1 Thompson magazine pouches for 20- and 30-round magazines (a few M1928A1 Thompsons remained in the units), the armored force helmet, map case (carried by tank officers), hip and shoulder holsters, and the early and late issue goggles (Resistol commercial goggles and the M1944 sun and sand goggle, the latter still in use to this day).

B: USMC LIGHT TANKS IN WORLD WAR II

The Marine Corps initially foresaw only the light tank in its doctrine for amphibious operations. Before the war, there were no modern medium tanks in the United States. Even the army light tanks found no official favor with Corps leaders, because of the limitations they saw in the capacities of navy landing craft and ships' cranes. The divisional tank battalions did not convert to all-medium tanks until the spring of 1944. Accordingly, the embryonic tank units of 1940–43 received a bewildering succession of light tanks from the supply chain as army-type light tanks first replaced the prewar Marmon-Herringtons, and then were replaced in turn by new types, models, and series as the American defense industry tooled up and produced improved tanks. Pictured are (period in service):

Marmon-Herrington CTL-3A (1936–42): The first tanks ordered for the Fleet Marine Force equipped the 1st Tank Company and later went to the 1st and 2d Scout Companies. They had high speed, weighed only 5 tons, and were armored against .30 caliber fire, sufficient for the kind of landings planned in the decade before the war.

M2A4 (1940–43): The first army-type light tank in USMC service, ordered when it became clear that the Marmon-Herrington Company could not produce CTL-type tanks fast enough for the new tank battalions ordered under the war emergency planning. But only 36 had been received when army production forced a shift to the M3 series. Only the A Companies of 1st and 2d Tank Battalions operated them, the former giving this tank its only combat operations. The shrouded recoil cylinder carried under the gun barrel best distinguishes it.

M3 (1941–43): Like the M2A4, the M3 provided machine-gun and 37mm fire in support of the infantry, considered sufficient for amphibious operations in 1940. The M3 offered marginal improvements in armor and a reduced ground pressure. The "hightop" or commander's cupola distinguishes this model, along with the sponson-mounted fixed machine guns. The 37mm recoil mechanism is now fully enclosed in the turret.

M3 hybrid (1941–42): Late-production M3s arrived in the two Marine Corps tank battalions without the "hightop" and with altered manual turret controls, features of the M3A1 incorporated prematurely into the M3 production line. Dubbed "flat-tops" or "hybrid" M3s, they were roundly disliked and prompted unit protests and investigations by the Marine Corps staff. They are identical to the M3A1 but retained the sponson machine gun mounts of the M3.

M3A1 (1942–44): The most numerous light tank in USMC service, the M3A1 introduced power traverse, improved periscopes, a turret basket, vertical gun stabilization, and more welding vice riveting. The cupola disappeared, replaced by a simple periscope. The Corps seemed at last to have found an effective weapon in series production.

M3A1 diesel (1942–43): Also arriving at the three tank battalions of 1942 were diesel-engine versions of the M3 and M3A1 series. Only the longer intake hoses on the engine deck distinguish these versions, extending forward from the air filter canisters to the forward part of the engine compartment, vice directly downward to the side of the canister.

M5A1 (1943–44): In order to reconcile the confusion resulting from the diffusion of M3, M3 hybrid and M3A1 tanks and diesel-engine versions of each, headquarters opted for a wholesale refit of the USMC divisional tank battalions in August 1942 with the M5A1 light tank. Improved in almost every respect, except for armament, the M5 entered service in the summer of 1943, but only with the 1st and 4th Tank Battalions, the 2d and 3d being too remote for a refit. But after the M5A1 operated in New Britain and Roi-Namur with these battalions, the decision had already been made to convert all the tank battalions to the medium tank, owing to the inadequacies of the 37mm gun; the M5A1 purchases were cancelled. The M5A1 is recognized by a totally redesigned upper hull and turret.

Pictured below are the standard 37mm munitions carried in the M2 through M5 tanks. Canister munitions are scaled-up shotgun shells, containing large round pellets. HE or high explosive ammunition contained an explosive charge with a point detonating fuse. APC and AP were solid steel armor-piercing projectiles, the former "capped" with a windscreen for higher velocity. TP was a training projectile, made of mild steel but a ballistic match to APC, and the drill cartridge was an inert dummy used to train loaders.

C: TRAINING SCENE

At New Caledonia, men throwing flour sacks simulate a Japanese close assault with explosives charges, catching the targeted M3A1 tank unawares. Fred Crowley watches helplessly from his driver's hatch as the "charges" arc toward his tank. In this drill, the tank crew is assigned a route to cover, and briefed that enemy stragglers have been spotted in the area. The crew is expected to observe the terrain all around the tank, using their vision ports and periscopes, and the driver is allowed to open his hatch as a safety measure. Other tankers of the same platoon or company form the "enemy" in the exercise. They hide singly or in pairs alongside the road, armed with the flour sacks. If they can approach the tank close enough to throw the sack against the turret or hull, they are considered to have made a "hit," destroying or disabling the tank.

In the first campaigns of the Marine Corps in the Pacific war, the Japanese deployed few antitank weapons, which normally consisted of 37mm antitank guns sited at important positions, such as airfields or major bases. Thus, the

The Japanese pole mine was used by a single soldier to attack a tank in close assault, usually causing his death in the resulting explosion. It consisted of one or more mines tied to a stout wood or bamboo pole of up to 10ft in length. (USMC photo)

greatest danger faced by the tankers was close assault by the Japanese infantrymen, who would throw themselves against the tank singly or in squads, using improvised explosives, bottled gasoline, or later the magnetic antitank mine or pole charge pictured above. The magnetic mine had a five- to six-second delay, but the pole charge was initiated by contact. Both devices usually killed the attacking infantryman as well. Japanese infantry doctrine emphasized the duty of a soldier to sacrifice himself to save the unit from enemy tanks, and the practice had been followed since the border fights with the Russians in 1937–39.

D: LEO CASE'S PLATOON AT THE BATTLE OF TENARU

Firing machine guns on the move and halting to fire canister rounds from their 37mm guns, these four M2A4 tanks of A Company, 1st Tank Battalion, mop up the survivors of the Ichiki Detachment, caught between the Tenaru and Ilu rivers on the north coast of Guadalcanal. Colonel Clifton B. Cates' 1st Marines routed the Ichiki Detachment, when the latter brazenly attacked the perimeter defenses from the east. At the end of the battle, the division commander authorized a tank attack, and a platoon of M2A4 tanks led by First Lieutenant Leo B. Case charged across the river's estuary into the coconut tree grove to annihilate the remnants before nightfall with 37mm and machine-gun fire. Apparently Case was jumping to get in to the action, and Colonel Cates finally let him go. Attacking without infantry support, since no tank–infantry doctrine yet existed in the Marine Corps, two tanks were eventually disabled, but the crews withdrew under covering fire of their platoon mates. As Bob Neiman later related, "Leo saw it as a field day as the Japanese had no antitank weapons. He spent an hour running over them with his tanks. One Japanese infantryman stopped a tank by jamming a bogey wheel with his rifle and it was disabled. Leo moved one tank at a time in to open a hatch and take one man at a time to the good tank, while three others circled to protect, repeated in sequence to get the crew out. Leo had no casualties, and continued in action. Finally Cates recalled

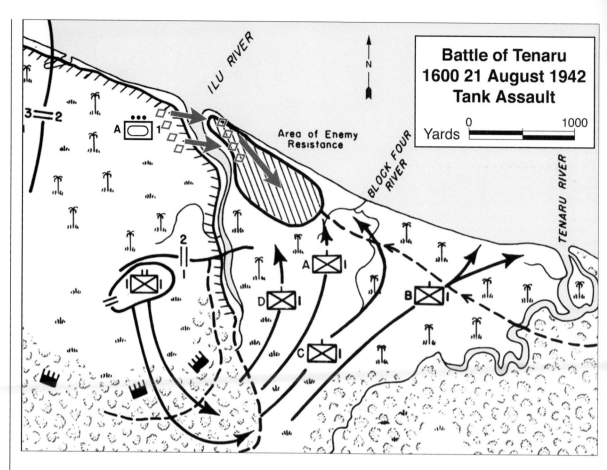

The map shows:

Battle of Tenaru
1600 21 August 1942
Tank Assault

Yards 0 — 1000

ILU RIVER

BLOCK FOUR RIVER

TENARU RIVER

Area of Enemy Resistance

3=2

A 1

2

A

D

B

C

N

The Battle of Tenaru saw the only clear success by USMC tanks in the Guadalcanal Campaign. The Ichiki Detachment had rashly crossed the Tenaru River to attack the lines of the 1st Marine Regiment, drawn up on the shore of the Ilu River. The Japanese were hemmed in against the shore and laced by fire from infantry, mortars, and artillery. The four M2A4 tanks administered the coup de grace. (Map by W. Stephen Hill from US Army original)

him with the radio and he said, 'I'm too busy killing Japs,' and stayed there, as he was that kind of a guy. But Cates took it OK and didn't court martial him and said later that he'd recommend him for a Navy Cross." Case later received the medal, the first tanker so recognized. He eventually commanded the 7th Tank Battalion when the Corps organized it in the Korean War expansion.

E: DAILY LIFE

In a break during the fight for Parry Island, in the Eniwetok Atoll, tankers of the 2d Separate Tank Company load ammunition near the beach, a few thousand yards behind the lines. There was no need to refuel, thanks to their twin General Motors diesel engines in the M4A2. The 75mm ammo came packed two to a box, each round packaged in a fiber cylinder. Usually with one man on guard, the other four work to strip the rounds of their packaging, laying them out on a canvas tarp. After checking for any imperfections,

loose fuses, or dirt, the four men load the rounds as well as boxes of machine gun ammo. The fifth man stows the rounds inside the turret and hull. Platoons usually worked in relays, so that the company continued to support its infantry regiment, in this case the 22d Marines. Once rearmed, the platoon leader would radio the company commander for the next assignment or return to the previously supported unit. The work is hot and crews frequently stripped down to essentials, and then donned the rest of their clothing to return to action. Here we see a typical admixture of camouflage and P1941 HBT-type utilities. They carry their pistols and pistol belts with magazine pouches only and have left all their other gear in the tank. The ammunition for the 75mm has the same projectile color system as the 37mm, in this case black for armor piercing, olive drab for high explosive, blue for training and gray for white phosphorus (none in 37mm) rounds. Amphibious assaults proved complex and chaotic in the execution and the resupply of tank ammo frequently failed. On Tarawa, tankers resorted to using pack howitzer rounds for the few M4A2s in action there. At Roi-Namur, a bigger surprise greeted Captain Bob Neiman: "We were low on ammo and sent a working party back to Roi to look for more, and all they could find was a cargo of practice ammo. In all my time in the Marine Corps I never saw any practice ammunition, but there on Roi, that was what had been landed. So we consolidated and redistributed ammo."

F: BATTLE SCENE, TINIAN, JULY 25, 1944

This view shows what the Japanese defenders on Tinian saw advancing toward them the day after the landing. The 2d Platoon, C Company, 2d Tank Battalion, advances across the cut cane fields, followed at a distance by riflemen of the 6th Marines. Unlike their distant cousins of the army fighting in Europe, the Marine Corps tanks go into action "buttoned up," because the main danger was a surprise assault by Japanese infantrymen, not enemy tanks. This practice had its dangers: it made it difficult to identify the occasional antitank guns firing from caves or camouflaged positions, and the Japanese garrisons of the islands closer to Japan had the 47mm gun, which could penetrate the sides of the M4 series medium tank. But the accompanying infantry had the responsibility not only to guard against enemy infantry attack, but also to alert the tankers to antitank guns and other dangers that they could see more clearly. Tinian was ideal tank terrain, rarely encountered in the Pacific war, and the advance went rapidly from north to south in a week. By the summer of 1944, all the Marine Corps divisions had worked out similar tank–infantry tactics, which did not exist earlier in the war. Squads closely accompanied tanks in a procedure called "physical protection," able to talk to the crew on the tank–infantry telephone or use hand and arm signals to indicate enemy positions. They could also flush out enemy antitank teams before they could attack their tanks. In more open terrain, where fewer hides existed for antitank teams, the procedure of "support by fire" required a squad of riflemen to watch over each tank and shoot down any Japanese infantrymen.

However, this more distant method prevented direct communications with the tanks, because the infantry and tank radios operated on different frequency bands.

G: AFTER THE BATTLE; STANDING DOWN

Here, Fred poses with his crew in September 1945, shortly before he rotated home on "points," the overseas service credits that determined the priority for discharge. The POA-CWS-H5 flame tank symbolizes the tremendous leap in combat capability and power that the tank arm of the Marine Corps had experienced since the war began. From the diminutive Marmon-Herringtons and naïve concepts of amphibious landings, the tank emerging at war's end was now a powerful 35-ton medium, armed with a 75mm cannon and coaxial flame gun, protected by up to 3.6in. of armor, all required for battle at close quarters with a hardened, tenacious foe.

All the men appear quite jaunty and giddy over surviving the war, and the way they are dressed shows it. P1941 utilities and cap, late-pattern coverall with garrison cap, and no shirt – this mixture passed as the uniform of the day in the late summer heat. For the Marine Corps ground troops, the Pacific war ended with the Battle of Okinawa and the beginning of summer, 1945. The Japanese surrender cancelled the two massive invasions planned for the Japanese home islands. Three Marine divisions would each have invaded Kyushu (scheduled for November 1945) and Honshu (March 1946). For the men of the 2d and 5th Tank Battalions, occupation duty in Sasebo became their next task, while 3d and 4th Tank Battalions disbanded and the tankers of 1st and 6th Tank Battalions accompanied their divisions to Shanghai and Tientsin. Occupation duty lasted barely a year, and the 5th Tank Battalion disbanded to join the remaining men of the 2d before all went home in 1946. The troops in north China were home in another year, and the greatly expanded Marine Corps of World War II had disappeared. For Fred and his tank crew, Sasebo was easy duty, and they used their new flame tank to dispose of the considerable Japanese war material at the naval base.

This POA-CWS-H5 flame tank of the 2d Tank Battalion is destroying Japanese aircraft collected at Sasebo Naval Air Station during its brief occupation duty in 1945–46. (USMC photo)

Figures in **bold** refer to illustrations

Bale, Capt Ed 45–46, 52, 59
Barrett, Brig-Gen Charles D. 27
Battalion, 1st Defense 22
battalions, Tank
  1st **10**, **14**, **18**, 25–26, **43**, 43, **44**, 56, 58, **63**, 63, **B**
    A Co. **11**, **23**, **24**, 31, 43, **D**
    B Co. 4, 8, 31, 41, 42, **57**
    C Co. 16–17, 31, 32, 43
  2d **16**, 16, **21**, 51–52, **52**, **63**, 63
    A Co. 4, **11**, 11–12, 17, 26, 43, 52, 53, **G**
    B Co. 11, **12**, 12, 18, **19**, 47–48, **48**
    C Co. 31, 41, 45, 46, **F**
  3d 16, 29, **46–47**, 49–50, 55
    B Co. **13**
  4th 24, 30, 43, 46, 54, 55, **B**
    C Co. **46–47**, 46, **49**, **53**, **54**, 54–55, **58**
  5th 13, 30, 52, 54, 55, **56**, 63
  6th 30, 52, **53**, 58, 59, 63
  organization 6
battle experience 31–32, 41 *see also* fight, learning to; tankers, veteran
Blanchard, Lt-Col John 41
Bougainville **13**, 41, 43

Camp Elliott, California **12**, 12–13, 24–25, **25**, 28, 29, 45 *see also* "Jacques' Farm"; training, Tank School
Camp New River (later Camp Lejeune), North Carolina 11, 25–26, 28, 29, 58
Camp Pendleton, California 30–31
"Camp Tarawa", Hawaii (Parker Ranch camp) 51–52
Case, 1st Lt Leo B. **D**
casualties 58–59
Cates, Col Clifton B. 32, **D**
China 58, **63**, 63
Civilian Conservation Corps (CCC) 7
clothing, combat 21–22, **22**, **G** *see also* uniforms
Collins, Maj William R. "Rip" 12–13
communications 20–21, 29, 45, 52–53, **A**
companies, Tank
  1st 27, 28, **B**
  1st Separate **18**
  2d and 3d 28
  2d Separate **42**, 43–44, **E**
  4th 28, **44–45**
Cook, Maj Jesse 11–12
Corps, III and V Amphibious 53, 56
Crowley, PFC (later Sgt) Fred 4, 17, 20, 21, 24, 25, 26, 52
  early life and enlistment 7–8
  training 9, 11, 12
  in New Caledonia 41–42, 44, 45, 48–49, 51–52, **C**
  aftermath 57–58, **G**

Dever, 2d Lt Joseph **18**
divisions, Marine
  1st 25, 30, 31, 50, 51, 53, 55–56
  2d 4, 30, 31, 53, 58
  3d 31, 51
  4th 16, 17, 31, 51
  5th 52, 58
  6th 30, 47–48, **48**, 51, 53, 55, **F**

7th 31
9th 55

English, Sgt (later Capt) Gearl M. "GM" 12, 14, 59
Eniwetok Atoll **6**, **42**, 44, **E**
equipment 8, 20, **22**, **A** *see also* footwear
  goggles **9**, **18**, 20, **58**, **A**
  helmets **9**, **17**, **18**, 20, **54**, **58**, **A**

fight, learning to 41–49 *see also* battle experience
flamethrower tanks 5, 57
  M3A1 "Satan" **16**, **48**, 49
  POA-CWS-H5 (M4-based) 54, **63**, **G**
Fleet Marine Force (FMF) 4, 10, 13–14, 26, 27
footwear **19**, 19, **22**, 58

Guadalcanal 5, 16, 31, 32, **51**
Guam 44–45, **46–47**, 49–50, 51

Iceland **11**, **17**, 26
infantry, marine **49**
Inks, 1st Sgt R. R. 8
Iwo Jima 5, 19, 22, **53**, 53–55, **54**, **56**, 59

"Jacques' Farm" 13, 14, 28–29, 30 *see also* Camp Elliott, California
Japanese army, Ichiki Detachment **62**, **D**
Jewell, Cpl 54

Korea 59
Kwajalein Islands, Battle for 43, **E**

landing ships, tank (LST) 41
life, daily **E**
lighter, 45ft tank **17**

Maui, Hawaii 51
McCard, Gunnery Sgt Bob 24, 49, 59
McMillian, Gunner (later 2d Lt) William Franklin 45–46, 52, 59
munitions **B**, **D**

Neiman, Capt (later Maj) Robert M. "Bob" **9**, 14, 16–17, 46, 54–55, **D**, **E**
Nevada, USS 8
New Caledonia **18**, 41–42, **C**

officers **9**, 9–10, **22**
Okinawa, Battle of 5, **53**, 53, 55–57, **57**, 59

Parris Island, South Carolina, training depot 7, 25
Parry Island, Eniwetok Atoll **6**, **E**
Pavavu, Russell Islands 51
pay scale 9
Peleliu **23**, **50**, 50–51, **51**
Pierson, 2d Lt Dick 16–17
Pugsley, Gunner Benjamin W. 32

Quantico, Virginia 9–10, 25, 28

rank structure 9
recovery vehicle, M32B2 tank **46–47**
Regiment, 1st Marine **62**, **D**
rest and recovery 51–52, **52**
Richards, Capt 4
Richert, Sgt 32
Roi-Namur, Battle for 43, **E**

Saipan, Mariana Islands 24, 44, 45–49, **48**, 51
Samoa **12**, 12, **18**, 18, 41, 43–44
San Diego, California, training depot 7, 13–14
Sasebo 57–58, **63**, **G**
Shepherd, Col (later Maj-Gen) Lemuel 5, 9–10
Stuart, Lt-Col Arthur J. 56–57
Sweeney, 2d Lt Robert J. 31
Swencesky, Capt Alexander 11, 45, 59

Tanambogo Island 31, 32
tank park routine 28–29
tanker, USMC **A**
tankers, veteran 49–57
tankette, Japanese Type 94: **58**
tanks, USMC 15, 26–28 *see also* flamethrower tanks
  Japanese Type 95 light **6**, 44, **46–47**, 50
  M2A4 light 5, **10**, **11**, 11, 15, **17**, 26, 27, 28, 32, 44–45, **B**, **D**
  M3 light 5, 11, **12**, 14, 15, **21**, **28**, 28, 29, 31, 32, **B**
    "flat-top" 29, **B**
  M3A1 **13**, **14**, 29, 31, 32, 41, **43**, **B**, **C**
  M4 medium 5, **19**, **54**, 57
  M4A1 **24**, 43
  M4A2 14, 15, **16**, **3**, 41, **42**, **43**, 43, **44–45**, **46–47**, **51**, **57**, **58**, **E**
    C22 "Comet" 44–45, 48–49, **52**
    dozer variant **44–45**, **51**, **53**
  M4A3 15, 52–53, **53**, 57
  M4A4 14, 41
  M5A1 light 15, **16**, 43, **44**, **B**
  M1917A1 light 4, 15, 26
  Marmon-Herrington 32, 41
    CTL-3 5, 10, 15, 26–28
    CTL-3A **4**, 27–28, **B**
    CTL-6 15, **18**, 28
    CTM-3TBD 15, **18**, 28
  protection, additional 46, **47**, **53**, **54**
  serial numbers 28
  T26 medium 57
Tarawa atoll 16, 41–42, **43**, 43, 44, **E**
Tenaru, Battle of **62**, **D**
Thomas, Maj Gerald 10
Tinian, Battle for 49, **52**, **F**
tractor, LVY-1 amphibious **4**
training 7, 8, 10–14, 16–17, 23, **C**
  marksmanship 8–9
  officers 9–10
  Tank School 12–14, 30 *see also* Camp Elliott; "Jacques' Farm"
training depots 7, 8, 13–14, 25 *see also* Camp Elliott
Tulagi Islands 31
Twining, Maj Merrill 10

uniforms *see also* clothing, combat; footwear
  Pacific war **18**, 18–21, **19**, **22**, **58**, **A**, **D**
  prewar **17**, 17–18, **21**
units, tank 13
Ushijima, Lt-Gen Mitsuru 5

Wake Island 22
weapons
  crew 8, **18**, **22**, **58**, **A**
  Japanese 46, **61**, **C**, **F**
  tank 29, 45, 48 *see also* munitions

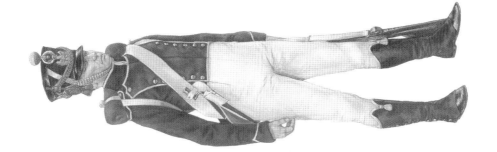

OSPREY
PUBLISHING

FIND OUT MORE ABOUT OSPREY

❑ Please send me the latest listing of Osprey's publications

❑ I would like to subscribe to Osprey's e-mail newsletter

Title / rank

Name

Address

City / county

Postcode / zip   state / country

e-mail

WAR

I am interested in:

❑ Ancient world

❑ Medieval world

❑ 16th century

❑ 17th century

❑ 18th century

❑ Napoleonic

❑ 19th century

❑ American Civil War

❑ World War 1

❑ World War 2

❑ Modern warfare

❑ Military aviation

❑ Naval warfare

Please send to:

North America:
Osprey Direct , 2427 Bond Street, University Park, IL 60466, USA

UK, Europe and rest of world:
Osprey Direct UK, P.O. Box 140, Wellingborough, Northants, NN8 2FA, United Kingdom

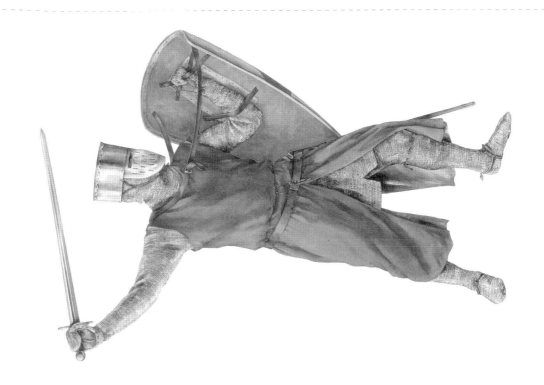

OSPREY
PUBLISHING

www.ospreypublishing.com

call our telephone hotline
for a free information pack

USA & Canada: 1-800-826-6600
UK, Europe and rest of world call:
+44 (0) 1933 443 863

Young Guardsman
Figure taken from *Warrior 22:
Imperial Guardsman 1799–1815*
Published by Osprey
Illustrated by Richard Hook

Knight, c.1190
Figure taken from *Warrior 1: Norman Knight 950 – 1204 AD*
Published by Osprey
Illustrated by Christa Hook

POSTCARD